Bloom's
GUIDES

Mary Shelley's
Frankenstein

CURRENTLY AVAILABLE

The Adventures of Huckleberry Finn
All the Pretty Horses
Animal Farm
Beloved
Beowulf
Brave New World
The Catcher in the Rye
The Chosen
The Crucible
Cry, the Beloved Country
Death of a Salesman
Fahrenheit 451
Frankenstein
The Glass Menagerie
The Grapes of Wrath
Great Expectations
The Great Gatsby
Hamlet
The Handmaid's Tale
The House on Mango Street
I Know Why the Caged Bird Sings
The Iliad
Jane Eyre

Lord of the Flies
Macbeth
Maggie: A Girl of the Streets
The Member of the Wedding
The Metamorphosis
Native Son
Of Mice and Men
1984
The Odyssey
Oedipus Rex
One Hundred Years of Solitude
Pride and Prejudice
Ragtime
The Red Badge of Courage
Romeo and Juliet
Slaughterhouse-Five
The Scarlet Letter
Snow Falling on Cedars
A Streetcar Named Desire
The Sun Also Rises
A Tale of Two Cities
The Things They Carried
To Kill a Mockingbird
The Waste Land

Bloom's
GUIDES

Mary Shelley's
Frankenstein

Edited & with an Introduction
by Harold Bloom

BLOOM'S
LITERARY CRITICISM
An imprint of Infobase Publishing

Bloom's Guides: Frankenstein

Bloom's Literary Criticism
An imprint of Infobase Publishing
132 West 31st Street
New York NY 10001

Library of Congress Cataloging-in-Publication Data
Mary Shelley's Frankenstein / [edited by] Harold Bloom.
    p. cm. — (Bloom's guides)
  Includes bibliographical references and index.
  ISBN-13: 978-0-7910-9358-0
  ISBN-10: 0-7910-9358-1
  1. Shelley, Mary Wollstonecraft, 1797–1851. Frankenstein. 2. Horror tales, English—History and criticism. 3. Frankenstein (Fictitious character) 4. Scientists in literature. 5. Monsters in literature. I. Bloom, Harold. II. Title: Frankenstein.

  PR5397.F73M38 2007
  823'.7—dc22   2007010199

Contributing Editor: Janyce Marson
Cover design by Takeshi Takahashi
Printed in the United States of America
Bang EJB 10 9 8 7 6 5 4 3 2 1
This book is printed on acid-free paper.

Contents

Introduction

HAROLD BLOOM

Frankenstein; or, The Modern Prometheus is the full title of Mary Wollstonecraft Godwin Shelley's inaugural science fiction novel, which she began before she was nineteen and finished less than a year later. Mary Shelley's full name is as important to understanding *Frankenstein* as is the book's full title. The novel intends us to see its protagonist, Dr. Victor Frankenstein, as the modern Prometheus, stealing creative fire from heaven in order to make a creature, a New Adam, whom most of us now call "the monster," because we have seen so many motion picture versions of *Frankenstein*. Despite his crimes, the creature is as much angel as monster, and we do best by following the book in calling him "the daemon." This ill-starred daemon is, in certain respects, a critique of all three illustrious figures who meet in Mary Shelley's full name: her mother, the radical feminist Mary Wollstonecraft; her father, the radical philosopher William Godwin; and her husband, the revolutionary lyrical poet Percy Bysshe Shelley. These three great idealists all had envisioned a new humanity in a newly structured society, and all had hoped that human nature could be redesigned, so as to eliminate exploitation, timidity, remorse, and conventional morality. Though Mary Shelley, to some extent, shared in these aspirations, her book nevertheless is a powerful, implicit critique of the Romantic Prometheanism of her husband and the radical rationalism of her parents.

The center of *Frankenstein* is the bitter relationship between Victor Frankenstein and his daemon, best expressed by the daemon when he cries out to the scientist: "Remember that I am thy creature; I ought to be thy Adam, but I am rather the fallen angel, whom thou drivest from joy for no misdeed." This alludes to the novel's epigraph, Adam's lament to God in John Milton's epic, *Paradise Lost*.

Did I request thee, Maker, from my clay
To mould me man? Did I solicit thee
From darkness to promote me?

One way to measure the vast distance between Mary Shelley's daemon and the movies' monster is to try to imagine any one of the film monsters educating himself by reading Milton's *Paradise Lost*. Mary Shelley's formidable daemon does exactly that, and receives a superb education in consequence. Unlike Victor Frankenstein, who is a literalist lacking in imagination, the daemon has the sensibility of an authentic poet. Critics tend to agree that Frankenstein and the daemon are the two halves of the same being, divided against itself. This gives an ironic sanction to the universal popular "error," by which the name of Frankenstein has come to mean the poor monster rather than its irresponsible creator. When we realize that, in the book, the creature is far more sympathetic than its maker, then we approach the heart of Mary Shelley's critique of the two men she loved best, her father and her husband, and of the mother whom she never knew, since Mary Wollstonecraft died in giving birth to the author of *Frankenstein*.

Though *Paradise Lost* is so crucial an influence upon *Frankenstein*, the novel's genre more closely resembles Jacobean revenge tragedy. What Frankenstein and his daemon ultimately desire is revenge upon one another. Each might say, with one of the revengers in John Webster's *The White Devil*: "I limned this night-piece, and it was my best." The book's final night-piece is its best, as Frankenstein and his daemon seek their final confrontation in an Arctic frozen sea. And yet the entire book is a night-piece, since it represents the torments of a civil war in the Promethean psyche, fought out between Frankenstein and his daemon. The daemon is superior to his maker both in spirit and in feeling, and so we come both to love him and to fear him. We do not have any particular affect towards the scientist who has both botched his work (the daemon is hideous in appearance) and failed to take responsibility for his creature. It is one of Mary Shelley's many fine ironies that the daemon mourns his dead maker, hardly an emotion that Victor

Frankenstein would have experienced had he succeeded in slaying his creation.

The relevance, aesthetic and moral, of Mary Shelley's novel only augments as we enter more deeply into an era that already has brought us "virtual reality" and seems likely to confront us with cyborgs. Victor Frankenstein, though he possesses generous impulses, is nothing less than a moral idiot in regard to the "monster" he has created. Even at the end, he cannot understand his own failure of moral imagination, and he dies still misapprehending the nature of his guilt. He is thus at once a great Hermetic scientist, an astonishing genius at breaking through human limitations, and a pragmatic monster, the true monster of the novel. His trespass is beyond forgiveness, because he is incapable of seeing that he is both a father, and a god, who has failed to love his marred creation. The novel's greatest strength seems to me its ironic contrast between the deepening of self-consciousness in the poor daemon and the narrowing of self-awareness in Victor Frankenstein. There are no victors in Mary Shelley's plangent novel: Frankenstein and the daemon both end in defeat. Yet the daemon has a tragic splendor, while Frankenstein is at most a figure of pathos. Our current purveyors of "third wave" future shock, and their political allies, ought to ponder the deeper meanings of Mary Shelley's Promethean parable.

Biographical Sketch

Mary Godwin was born in London, England, on August 30, 1797, the daughter of William Godwin, the writer and philosopher, and his feminist activist wife, Mary Wollstonecraft. Tragically, Mary Wollstonecraft died of puerperal fever eleven days after giving birth to her daughter. Wollstonecraft, the author most famous for her *Vindication of the Rights of Woman with Strictures on Political and Moral Subjects* (1792), argued for the rightful education and value of women. By the time of Mary's birth, William Godwin had already written *An Enquiry Concerning Political Justice* (1793), advocating a republican and minimal form of government, and a novel, *Caleb Williams* (1794), a fictional attack on current social values. Both Wollstonecraft and Godwin lent their voices to the revolutionary passions of their day and rejected the status quo.

Mary Godwin's life was difficult from the outset. On December 21, 1801, her father remarried and Mary Jane Clairmont became her stepmother. The new Mrs. Godwin was obnoxious and unethical, opening people's mail, acting behind their backs, and slandering them. Try as she might, she could not love Mary, and Mary would forever resent her stepmother, accusing her of taking her father away. Her stepmother also succeeded in removing all other members of the household whom the young Mary had come to love, including her nursemaid and Wollstonecraft's former maid. Godwin's friends felt bad for Mary. As a result of this union, Mary Godwin inherited a household consisting of Fanny Imlay (the daughter of Mary Wollstonecraft by Gilbert Imlay), and a stepsister and stepbrother, Jane (later called Claire) and Charles Clairmont.

Mary Godwin was educated at home by her father according to his principles of the cultivation of knowledge and feelings through the liberal arts, which he had studied at the Dissenting schools. His instruction was rigorous and ambitious, his primary interests being history and literature, the Latin and Greek classics, and Shakespeare, Milton, and other first-rate poets of every language. He likewise encouraged his daughter in literary pursuits. Indeed, Godwin published Mary's light verses. "Mounseer Nongtongpaw" was published in 1808 and was later pirated in the United States. Her enduring mythological hero was Prometheus, the same god whose name becomes the subtitle for *Frankenstein*. Mary was also given considerable access to the intellectual reading matter in Godwin's own library. Another important part of her education consisted of family outings to lectures, theaters, and other events in London. Finally, her education was greatly enhanced by a multitude of visitors to the Godwin residence, including Wordsworth, the painters Thomas Lawrence and James Northcote, the actor-manager Charles Kemble, the scientist Humphrey Davy, and Maria Edgeworth, to name just a few luminaries.

On July 28, 1814, Mary Godwin, only seventeen years of age, and the radical poet-philosopher, Percy Bysshe Shelley, twenty-one at the time, decided to elope to France, a country still recovering from defeat in war. Their actions were considered scandalous. Besides the fact that they were not married, Shelley was still married to another woman, Harriet Shelley. Their passion and sexual attraction were overwhelming and, when William Godwin became aware of the relationship, he argued with his daughter about her affair. By the time they eloped, Mary was already pregnant by Shelley, a situation rendered even more scandalous by Shelley's desertion of Harriet, who was also pregnant. Godwin refused to communicate with his daughter for a period of more than two years. However, given her parents' personal histories, her father's admonition failed to deter her. When she left with Shelley for a tour of continental Europe, they took their companion, Mary's stepsister Jane Clairmont, with them. Jane too wished to get away from her mother's ever-watchful eye and, given her reading of romances and ghost stories, she longed to travel. Furthermore, Jane had been the agent for arranging secret meetings for the lovers in the weeks leading up to their elopement. Once in Paris, they settled into cheap lodgings at the Hôtel de Vienne while planning a journey to Switzerland. The three had left behind many distressed relatives, among them Percy's wife who was pregnant with their second child, Charles Shelley, while caring for their daughter, Ianthe Shelley. The list of unhappy family members also included Mary's stepmother, who rushed to Calais in an attempt to dissuade her daughter, and William Godwin, who, despite his radical views, was concerned about the notoriety that this unconventional marriage would bring to his daughter.

Mary had met Percy less than two years prior to their marriage when the poet paid a visit to the Godwin household. Godwin was in a great deal of business debt and Shelley, who had pledged to pay the totality of Godwin's indebtedness over time, had come over to discuss the terms of a loan they were negotiating with a Mr. Nash. When his business discussion with Godwin was concluded, Shelley visited Mary at her schoolroom to discuss politics and women's rights. Before he left for home a few days later, Shelley bought Mary a notebook to use for a translation of the *Aeneid* she was about to begin. The two were falling in love, though Percy was still married. At the time of his first visit to the Godwin's, Percy was accompanied by his wife, Harriet Shelley, who despite her education was deemed by her husband to be one-dimensional. When Shelley's father later insisted that his son give up his radical views as the condition for financial assistance, the poet refused and the relationship with his wife became even more difficult. The couple separated and it was rumored that Harriet was having an affair with a certain Captain Ryan who, it was further rumored, was the biological father of her second child, Charles. Percy Shelley never knew for sure, but went on the assumption that the child was his as it would have been financially disadvantageous for him not to be the actual father.

Both prior to and following her introduction to Percy, Mary had been living in Scotland, where she was introduced to Scottish traditions and myths and was encouraged to write stories. She delved into the occult aspects of Scottish culture and became enamored of its legends, including dealings with the devil, the raising of spirits, and humanoid monsters. At this time, Mary's favorite older poets were Spenser, Sidney,

Shakespeare, and Milton, while Wordsworth, Coleridge, South, and Byron were her favorite modern poets. She had met Shelley during a brief return home to London and soon returned to Scotland with her traveling companion, Isabella Baxter. During her sixteen months at the spacious Baxter residence, Mary was able to live according to her own values: privacy, intellectual and loving companionship, and a close proximity with nature. When she next met Percy on May 5, 1814, he was estranged from his wife, and fell in love with Mary, whom he described as "a child of love and light." He admired Mary for her bold and fearless ways as well as her knowledge and interest in abstruse subjects. It should be noted that Mary's name and parentage were an additional allure for the handsome young poet. For her part, Mary loved Shelley as the living embodiment of her parents' radical ideals. Percy was dedicated to human betterment and great generosity, sentiments for which Mary had a great deal of sympathy. Added to these attractive qualities, Shelley was also an accomplished classical scholar.

While traveling in Switzerland with Percy and Jane, Mary Shelley wrote her *History of a Six Weeks' Tour* (published in 1817), a record of her response to the grandeur of the Alps with a vision that appreciated the vital and life-giving elements among the frozen wastes, in a word, the sublime. "The scenery of this day's journey was divine, exhibiting piny mountains barren rocks, and spots of verdure surpassing imagination." And at the desolate summit of Montanvert, she surveyed the barren ice-fields in order to discover how the meager forms of life struggled to survive. "We went on the ice; it is traversed by irregular crevices.... The air is very cold, yet many flowers grow here, and, among others, the rhododendron, or *Rose des Alpes*, in great profusion."

During the eight years of the Shelleys' life together, they were often on the move, with stints in England, France, Italy, and elsewhere, occasionally moving homes several times a year. Their family situation was complex—between 1815 and 1819, Mary lost three of her four children. In February 1815, Mary's first child, a daughter, was born prematurely and died several days later. In January 1816, her son William was born, but he died three years later. Then, in September 1817, a third child was born, Clara, who died in 1818. Their fourth child, a son named Percy Florence, was born on November 12, 1819. During this same period, Fanny Imlay and Harriet Shelley committed suicide, replacing the cold intellectual life of Mary's youth with misery and death. In addition to their domestic problems, the Shelleys both worked hard, reading widely and writing assiduously. They mixed with a number of the most significant cultural figures of the times, in particular Lord Byron. It was during this period, and at only eighteen years of age, that Mary's first and most famous work, *Frankenstein*, was famously composed as a result of a ghost story competition during a long, wet summer in Geneva. The family drama found in *Frankenstein* (first published in 1818) is a work incorporating many details from her familial experiences and disappointments as well as her unique education and acquaintance with some of the most gifted writers and thinkers of her time. Indeed, each unit in the novel, from the explorer's paternal reverence of Victor Frankenstein to Victor's own tortured relationship with his creation, represents a familial bond, ruptured or otherwise. In *Frankenstein* Mary Shelley succeeded not only in creating an enduring myth but also in expressing the dangers of driving scientific activity to its limits without considering the possible human consequences. Ultimately, Mary's fascination with scientific radicalism in the book brought her criticism and she was forced to bowdlerize her own book for later editions.

Early in June 1822, Mary suffered a miscarriage and only survived because Percy immediately immersed her in a bath of freezing water to staunch the bleeding. On July 8, 1822, the final tragedy of their marriage took place when Percy Bysshe and Edward Williams drowned during a storm while on a boating trip. The boat they were on was new and had been christened the Don Juan by Byron. It was a defining moment for Mary. The consequence of Percy's untimely death left a burden of guilt, and Mary was determined to alleviate her trauma by publishing Shelley's poems and writing his biography. From this point forward, Mary Shelley was driven to write different fictionalized versions of her life with Percy. However, her plans to write a formal biography of her husband never came to fruition, most especially in that she could never have gotten her father to sanction it. On October 2, 1822, Mary began to write what she referred to as her "Journal of Sorrow" in which she approached the painful subject of the terms on which she and Percy had parted and, in so doing, constructed a romantic fiction, a story that was happy yet troubled:

> For eight years I communicated with unlimited freedom with one whose genius, far transcending mine, awakened & guided my thoughts ... Now I am alone! Oh, how alone.... How often during those happy days, happy though chequered, I thought how superiorly gifted I had been in being united to one whom I could unveil myself, & who could understand me.

In June 1824, in an attempt to restore Percy's reputation before a largely hostile public, and after expending an enormous amount of editorial effort, Mary published the *Posthumous Poems of Percy Bysshe Shelley*. However, when Percy's father, Timothy Shelley, demanded that Mary relinquish custody of all manuscript material and that the book itself be suppressed or face the discontinuation of his financial support for Mary and his grandson, Mary capitulated to his ultimatum, withdrawing the 200 remaining copies.

The task of writing about Shelley's life continued in her next novel, *The Last Man* (published in 1826), which celebrated her experience as part of the very gifted and intellectual company of Shelley and Byron. The latter had died in April 1824 in Missolonghi during his attempt to aid the Greeks in their struggle for independence, although it was not until May that news of his death reached England. Mary reflected upon the untimely death of these two luminaries while she, a mere twenty-six years old, was "doomed to live on seeing all expire before her ... in the condition of an aged person," all her old friends having passed away. *The Last Man* takes place on a vast scale and moves through the destruction of humanity by war and plague until only one man remains. A far lesser work to the seminal *Frankenstein*, it is still affecting and conceptually powerful, a book not without its literary and cultural influences. First and foremost among those influences would be Byron himself. Prior to leaving Italy, Mary spent a good deal of time transcribing Byron's poetry in which she would have confronted his ideas on the decline of civilization, a notion that was influenced by his reading of the work of the French geologist Georges Cuvier. *The Last Man* may also have been influenced by the work of the German poet and dramatist, Johann Schiller, whom both the Shelleys had read. Schiller had prophesied the fragmentation of society in apocalyptic terms as "a patching together of a vast number of lifeless parts [from which] a collective mechanical life results" and Thomas Malthus's *Essay on the Principles of Population* in which the author warned of the catastrophic consequences that would result from the overpopulation of cities. Malthus's *Essay* first appeared in 1798, and by 1817 his work was in its fifth edition. Significantly, in *The Last Man*, the deaths of the Byron and Shelley characters, both of whom are portrayed as irremediably flawed, are not from the plague that wipes out the rest of humankind, but instead follow the tragedies of their real lives. At the time, like many of Mary Shelley's works, it was mocked on the grounds of its author's gender, "The Last Woman" being the cruel and chauvinistic title of one review.

Following Percy's death, the twenty-four-year-old Mary returned to England with her remaining child, Percy Florence. Money continued to be a constant problem, despite Percy Shelley's having been the heir to a rich baronetcy and Percy Florence in turn becoming heir in 1826 following the death of Percy Bysshe's elder half-brother Charles. Mary was by then earning her living as an early Victorian woman of letters, and she occasionally hovered on the brink of poverty. Added to her financial woes was Mary's scandalous past, which, despite the anxious conformity of manner in which she raised her son, continued to plague her so that she never became entirely assimilated into the middle-class mainstream. Finally, her depressive tendencies meant that she felt slights and social rejections more keenly, and these situations unfortunately far outweighed those friendships in which others were happy to accept her on her own terms. In the 1840s, Mary Shelley was subjected to two particularly cruel blackmail attempts. In 1845 an itinerant Italian political rebel, whom Mary had initially supported both emotionally and financially, attempted to extort money from her on the basis of some affectionate letters she had written to him. A year later, Thomas Medwin, an old friend of Shelley, threatened Mary with the publication of a life of Percy Bysshe that would expose some of the obfuscations and distortions Shelley's friends and admirers had considered necessary to win public recognition for the poet. In her later years, Mary's depression would prove to be exacerbated by an undiagnosed brain tumor. She died in 1851 at the home of her son and his wife.

The Story Behind the Story

The Circle of Friends at the Villa Diodati

Mary Shelley's *Frankenstein* was born of a waking nightmare she had on June 16, 1816. It was a vision so intense that it produced one of the most powerful horror stories in Western literature, a story that assumed mythic dimensions as it addressed profound implications concerning man's understanding of his place in the world and the consequences of transgressing against God and Nature. At the time *Frankenstein* was first conceived, Mary and Percy Bysshe Shelley were living outside Geneva at the Maison Chapuis, a cottage on the water at Cologny, and were visitors at the nearby Villa Diodati[1] where Lord Byron, Claire Clairmont, and Byron's physician, John Polidori, were living at the time. During the course of several days in June, the group was kept indoors by incessant rainfall. One evening, while they were sitting around reading some ghost stories, they each agreed to write their own horror tale. For several days, Mary tried to imagine such a story, but failed to come up with one. However, following a discussion between Shelley and Byron concerning galvanism and Erasmus Darwin,[2] Mary fell into a reverie in which she saw "the pale student of unhallowed arts kneeling beside the thing he had put together," namely, a hideous corpse that he had reanimated with a "spark of life." She finally had her ghost story.

Given the very unconventional group of friends assembled that June, it is no surprise that so uniquely fantastic a story as *Frankenstein* was conceived. Lord Byron, one of the most important figures of the Romantic movement, had already acquired a very scandalous reputation. Lady Byron left him amid horrendous rumors about his amatory experiences and Byron soon left London. However, before he left, Claire Clairmont pursued and seduced him while he was in the final stages of securing a legal separation from his wife. During this interval, she had a brief affair with Byron, who made it clear to her that it was over. Claire then persuaded the Shelleys to take her along with them to Geneva. When the group finally caught up with Byron, the latter was very displeased to see Claire once again. To further complicate matters, Claire then announced that she was pregnant and Percy had to intercede on her behalf to secure child support from Byron. For his part, during the summer of 1816, Byron was busy writing poetry, including the third canto of *Childe Harold*, which Mary cherished as it included their summer experience. Furthermore, Byron's personal physician, John Polidori, had accompanied Byron to Geneva. Polidori is reported to have been a genius as a medical doctor who, unfortunately, had an obsessive love for Lord Byron and a misguided belief that his close association with Byron and Shelley would be enough to prove his literary talents. Eventually, he was hired by Lord Byron, a poet for whom he had great admiration. As it turned out, Lord Byron, a confirmed hypochondriac, was more interested in the doctor's handsome appearance, and the two became lovers. Unfortunately, Byron became abusive and cruel in his ridicule of Polidori's writing skills and following their stay at the Villa Diodati, Byron dismissed him. During the next five years, Polidori made many suicide attempts. All of these events notwithstanding, his story, "The Vampyre," has been credited with influencing Bram Stoker's *Dracula*.

Frankenstein and His Monster: A Mechanical Exchange

The story of a scientific experiment with unanticipated consequences or a modern Prometheus transgressing the divine and inviolable secrets of human life, Victor Frankenstein and his creature, creator and daemon, are inextricably bound to each other and share the same fate. In his attempt to create life in a laboratory, Victor Frankenstein produces a quasi-mechanical being, frightening in aspect, yet possessing an incredible sensitivity and intellect. For the crime he has committed in crossing the boundaries of forbidden intelligence, and his subsequent attempts to conceal all knowledge and responsibility for what he has unleashed, Victor Frankenstein places himself, and his creature, beyond all possibility of redemption. Though we can identify the creator from his creation, it is not at all entirely clear what to make of them.

Victor is ostensibly a young man born into a nurturing family, albeit an unconventional one where stepchildren become spouses, while the male monster is something other than human, having been manufactured from dead human parts and animated by an electrical spark. Given the monster's morbid composition, his birth is strangely belated and has an after-the-fact quality to it since Victor cannot possibly imagine how this "birth" will turn out or the dire consequences that will result from it. Finally, the monster is often mistakenly referred to as Frankenstein, the name of his creator, eclipsing the fact that he is eternally nameless. Thus, the question remains as to the true nature of both the monster and his creator, for we cannot speak of them separately. The monster is Victor's daemon and, as such, is a manifestation of his divided personality. What follows is a discussion of an aesthetic paradigm, articulated by M.H. Abrams, that can be applied to gain a better understanding of their characterizations.

Following a discussion of eighteenth-century philosophical theories of art and reality, Abrams provides an outline of an aesthetic model that emerged from this school of thinking and that was then applied to the criticism of literary works.[3] This aesthetic model involved the metaphor of a plant, which provided a way to distinguish between two opposing concepts of the imagination—the organic and the mechanical. Abrams organizes the main features of that metaphor according to Samuel Taylor Coleridge's theory of literary invention. Though Coleridge's theory is elaborate and complex, there are some characteristics of the metaphor of the organism that can be applied to Victor Frankenstein and his daemon as a way to identify their true nature, an opposition of the human versus the mechanical being.

The essential properties of the organic or plant metaphor that would be useful here are that (a) the plant is an organism, originating from a seed, with the whole being greater than the sum of its parts; (b) as a natural entity, it necessarily grows and otherwise manifests productivity; (c) it evolves spontaneously from an internal source of energy; and (d) its structure is an organic unity with an innate and inviolable organization whereas a machine is merely a combination of materials whose parts can be substituted because it lacks an inherent and inviolable unity. In short, the difference between the plant and the machine hinges on the absolute possession or complete lack of an absolute integrity. The converse of these criteria is, of course, a definition of the mechanical imagination. Accordingly, an examination of Victor Frankenstein and his monster in light of this notion of an inviolable integrity, in both a physical and ethical dimension, can yield some important insights into their true nature.

From a physical standpoint, Victor is clearly human. The biological son of Alphonse and Caroline Frankenstein, he comes from a happy and nurturing family and, in growing up, is a sensitive, intelligent, and responsible child who begins his professional education at the University of Ingolstadt with an enthusiasm for the natural sciences. Unfortunately, it is also this enthusiasm that leads to his downfall as he becomes increasingly seduced by his own abilities to surpass all other scientists before him. The culmination of this seduction takes place at the moment he brings his creature to life. From that point onward, Victor Frankenstein's physical and mental well-being are disrupted and become increasingly unstable as he becomes steadily tormented and sickened by what he has wrought. More importantly, however, is his belief and abject fear that he must never disclose what he has done. Thus, he is forever enjoined from speaking the truth and, consequently, can never again act in an ethical manner. As a result of his experiment and the many transgressions it implies, including a usurping of God's authority, Victor Frankenstein forfeits his integrity. While he becomes increasingly speechless and otherwise incapable of communicating with others, the most extreme instance of his lack of integrity is his inability to testify on Justine's behalf and, thereby, becoming responsible for her execution.

In the case of the monster, he is truly a manufactured being who is haphazardly put together from body parts that Victor has collected from charnel houses. Indeed, he is a composite of dead matter that lacks any organizational plan, natural or otherwise, since Victor has no preconceived idea of how or whether the disparate parts will actually work. Victor simply learns as he goes along in the construction of his monster, making adjustments and modifications on an ad hoc basis. Thus the monster, created by artificial means in the laboratory and abandoned in the hour of his birth at the sight of his frightening aspect, is a being condemned to loneliness and rejection from all who look upon him. Yet the monster is a sentient being, demonstrating an aptitude for literary criticism as he interprets *Paradise Lost* and other classics as they relate to his status and teach him about mankind. But above all else, the monster develops into an eloquence, arguing persuasively and, at least temporarily, convincing Victor that he is obligated to fashion him a female companion. It is as though the monster has stolen Victor's powers of articulation and may likely have surpassed him as well since we have no real evidence of Victor's previous rhetorical skills. Furthermore, the monster plays on our sympathies and, although we cannot absolve him for the crimes he has committed and the chaos he has caused, we do understand his motives. Indeed, in those earlier moments when he acts out of love and a genuine desire to participate in the human community, the monster acts with integrity. In sum, the monster's acquisition of human qualities appears to be at the expense of Victor's dehumanization, thereby blurring the distinctions between the human and the mechanical being.

Notes

1. The Villa Diodati had its own claim to literary fame. John Milton had stayed at the villa, while Voltaire, Rousseau, Gibbon, and Madame de Stael had all resided on its shores.

2. Erasmus Darwin (1731–1802) was one of the founding members of the Lunar Society, a group of pioneering industrialists and natural philosophers. Darwin had succeeded in causing a piece of vermicelli to move via influence of an electrical current.

3. Abrams, M.H. *The Mirror and the Lamp: Romantic Theory and the Critical Tradition*. Oxford: Oxford University Press (1953): 167–174.

List of Characters

Victor Frankenstein is the protagonist of Mary Shelley's novel. As a young child he grows up in a nurturing environment and, along with his other studies, develops an interest in the occult scientists, which becomes an overwhelming passion when he arrives at the University of Ingolstadt. After he fashions a creature in his laboratory, Victor Frankenstein's fate is sealed. From that point forward, and despite all efforts to the contrary, he can no longer lead a productive or normal life. The pursuit of his creature becomes his only mission.

The "Monster" is an avenging spirit, a manifestation of Victor's divided psyche and, as such, can be deemed the other protagonist in *Frankenstein*. A composite of the parts of corpses collected during Victor Frankenstein's nocturnal visits to charnel houses and graveyards, he is brought to life by a spark of electricity. From the moment he is "born," Victor is horrified by his hideous appearance and attempts to flee, though the monster is determined to redress the terrible injustices done to him.

Elizabeth Lavenza Frankenstein is the niece and adopted daughter of Caroline and Alphonse Frankenstein who later marries Victor Frankenstein. A sweet and loving addition to the Frankenstein household, Elizabeth seals her fate in marrying Victor as she falls prey to the monster on her wedding night.

Justine Moritz is a servant in the Frankenstein household. She is a kind and loving young woman who is later framed, by the monster, and executed for the murder of the youngest of the Frankenstein children, William. Though Victor knows her to be innocent, he is enjoined from testifying for to do so would reveal his awful secret.

William Frankenstein is the youngest brother of Victor. The first of the monster's victims, William is found strangled in the forest near Geneva.

Ernest Frankenstein is another of Victor Frankenstein's younger brothers. A sickly child at birth, he plays a relatively minor role in the novel and remains the sole survivor of the Frankenstein family.

Alphonse Frankenstein is Victor's father, an amiable and virtuous man of character, who remains the eternal optimist despite the tragic loss he is forced to endure. He has a sincere and unfailing love for his son, and dismisses Victor's attempts to confess his sins—regarding these statements as a sign of sickness. Alphonse eventually succumbs to a broken heart following a series of tragic losses to the Frankenstein family.

Caroline Frankenstein is the kind devoted wife of Alphonse Frankenstein. Though she is the "adopted" daughter of Alphonse Frankenstein, she later becomes his wife. Selflessly devoted to her family, her premature death is the result of attending her niece, Elizabeth Lavenza, who was recovering from scarlet fever. Before she dies, she exacts a deathbed promise that Victor will one day marry Elizabeth.

Henry Clerval is the son of a merchant and a dear friend of Victor's. A sensitive and caring young man, he is Victor's close friend. When Victor begins to unravel at Ingolstadt, Clerval becomes his nurse and protector. Ultimately, he becomes one of the monster's victims.

M. Waldman is a professor at Ingolstadt, of whom Victor is very fond. Victor wanders into his lecture in which Waldman delivers an inspiring discussion of modern chemistry, acknowledging the importance of the ancient writers. Waldman becomes Victor's mentor and friend. He encourages Victor to study science and allows Victor to use the laboratory once he has advanced in his studies.

M. Krempe is a professor of natural history at the University of Ingolstadt. Victor takes an immediate dislike to Krempe's disagreeable personality and repulsive appearance, while Krempe is dismissive of the ancient writers that Victor admires, finding them unfit for the new enlightened and scientific age.

De Lacey is the patriarch of the De Lacey family whom the monster grows to love. A kindly old man from France, he is the father of Agatha and Felix. Though once prosperous and well-respected, he is now blind and living an impoverished life in Germany.

Robert Walton is a would-be poet turned explorer of the North Pole and the captain of his vessel. His crew rescues Victor from the icy sea and he becomes Victor's devoted friend, nursing him through his illness and honoring Victor's dying wish that he continue to pursue the monster. Walton's letters to his sister, Margaret Saville, frame the novel.

Agatha De Lacey is the mild-mannered and devoted daughter of the elderly De Lacey. The monster is immediately taken with Agatha and her brother, and is moved by their devotion to their father.

Felix De Lacey is the loving son of De Lacey. His concern and extraordinary efforts on behalf of the Turk are unreciprocated when the latter reneges on his promise to allow his daughter, Safie, to marry Felix.

Safie is the daughter of the Turkish merchant and the young woman with whom Felix is in love, referring to her as "his sweet Arabian." Safie, who is in love with Felix, escapes her father and travels a great distance to find Felix who by then is leading a life of hardship in Germany.

The Turk is a Turkish merchant in France and Safie's father. Though he is never actually named, he is shown to be duplicitous and self-serving. In order to save his own life, he promises to allow Felix to marry Safie, but reneges after he is set free.

Mr. Kirwin is a kindly Irish magistrate who takes care of Victor after he is accused of and imprisoned for the murder of Henry Clerval. Kirwin is responsible for delivering Victor safely back to his father.

Margaret Saville is Robert Walton's sister. Though she plays no part in the novel, Walton's letters, which record Victor's story, are addressed to her.

Summary and Analysis

VOLUME I
Robert Walton's Letters

The main narrative of *Frankenstein* is initiated and concluded by a series of letters from Robert Walton, an explorer and sea captain, who recounts the story of Victor Frankenstein to his sister, Margaret Saville. Robert, like Victor Frankenstein, is seized by an overzealous curiosity to explore uncharted territory, to "tread a land never before imprinted by the foot of man," referring to the North Pole. When the novel opens, dated St. Petersburgh, Dec. 11th, 17____ (**Letter I**), Walton, already at sea, is brimming with enthusiasm for his voyage, so much so that the icy breeze "fills him with delight." Nevertheless, as he admits to his sister, his enthusiasm is tempered by a degree of apprehension that his voyage may fail and that he may never see his sister again. Adding to these fears is his responsibility for his crew and the effort he must expend in keeping up their morale. All of the above notwithstanding, Walton's voyage is the fulfillment of a childhood dream to journey to an undiscovered place. It is also significant that Walton reveals another childhood passion to become a poet after reading works that "entranced his soul." "I imagined that I also might obtain a niche in the temple where the names of Homer and Shakespeare are consecrated." Regrettably, in the space of a year his talent for poetry proved disappointing, although he was soon redeemed by inheriting his cousin's fortune, enabling him to pursue yet another dream. At present, Walton's plans are going well, though his training has been difficult, accompanying whalers on expeditions to the North Sea while facing bitter cold and privation, while also having to study mathematics, medicine, and the physical sciences. With this training behind him, it is with great anticipation that he welcomes his travels in Russia, where the snow sleighs are the means of transportation. Walton concludes his first letter stating his plans to leave for Archangel in two week's time where he will hire a ship for the purpose of whaling.

Walton's second letter (**Letter II**) is written in March, from Archangel. He has now hired a vessel and is busy organizing sailors, whom he believes are fearless. But, despite his various preparations, Walton is depressed, longing for something even more important than his anticipated expedition, namely a sympathetic friend. At the time this letter is written, Walton is twenty-eight years old, lamenting the fact that he is self-educated, and expressing an earnest wish for a companion who is "cultivated" and in a position to offer him guidance when needed. "I desire the company of a man who can sympathize with me; whose eyes would reply to mine." Walton, however, is despondent about his ability to find such a soul mate, though he does mention a lieutenant whom he has employed and for whom he has a great deal of respect. "The master is a person of excellent disposition, and is remarkable in the ship for his gentleness and the mildness of his discipline.... He is, moreover, heroically generous." Walton then recounts how this exceedingly selfless lieutenant had fallen in love with, and planned to marry, a rich Russian lady when he learned that she was in love with someone else, whereupon he abandoned his marital plans and then left his entire fortune to his rival, a man much poorer than himself. As it turned out, the woman's father felt duty bound to honor the lieutenant's betrothal, at which point the lieutenant, having no other way out, left the country so that the two lovers could finally marry. While vowing never to tempt fate by killing an albatross (an allusion to Coleridge's "Rime of the Ancient Mariner"), this second letter concludes with Robert acknowledging the possibility that he may never again see his sister.

Letter III is a rather short one in comparison to the two preceding letters. It is written on July 7th, four months after the second one, and reaches his sister through a merchant who is bound homeward from Archangel. Though Walton longs to see his native land again, he writes about the determination of his crew. Resolute in their mission, they do not allow minor dangers to deter them. "[N]or do the floating sheets of ice that continually pass us, indicating the dangers of the region towards which we are advancing, appear to dismay them." It should also be noted that it is now the middle of summer and they have yet to encounter the anticipated dangers of the North Pole. This third letter is a reassuring one in which Walton attempts to allay his sister's fears (and probably his own as well) by suggesting that he and his crew have proven themselves competent in handling bad weather.

Letter IV consists of three separate letters, the first of which is written on August 5th and is markedly different from the reassuring mood of the prior letter, and begins by stating that the events he is about to record are a truly incredible story. It records Walton's first impressions of Victor Frankenstein and his monster—events that took place on the preceding Monday, July 31st. At that time, while heading into a frozen terrain "of vast and irregular plains of ice," Walton's crew, surveying their surroundings through a telescope, spot a being of enormous physique gliding rapidly across the ice upon a sleigh drawn by dogs. The following morning, Walton finds his crew talking to someone in the water who was floating on a sleigh sitting atop a large piece of ice, with only one dog still alive. The stranger, who appeared to be a European man, will later be identified as Victor Frankenstein. Most remarkable of all, however, is that though the stranger, shivering and sickly, is in great need of rescuing, he will only come aboard if he is told where the ship is headed. When told that they were destined for the "northern pole," the stranger was satisfied. Walton tells his sister that "[h]is limbs were nearly frozen, and his body dreadfully emaciated by fatigue and suffering. I never saw a man in so wretched a condition." Two days hence, the stranger began to recover and, despite his wild expression, seemed to Walton to be a gentle being. When the stranger learns that the crew saw the same gigantic being whom he is pursuing, he listens with rapt attention to all details concerning his "daemon," exhibiting an eagerness to stay on deck and watch for the sleigh to reappear. The letter ends with Walton declaring that the stranger is the friend whom he had hoped to meet, stating that he loved him as a brother.

The next letter, written on August 13th, begins with another declaration of Walton's great affection for his new "guest," a man for whom he feels both respect and compassion, one who spoke affectively and artfully. When Walton confesses to Victor that he is the very friend he hoped for, Victor begins to lament the loss of his cherished, childhood friend, "the most noble of human creatures." Nevertheless, despite the stranger's melancholy, Walton is duly impressed by his ability to find solace in nature. Though he does not know it at the time, Walton's observations are shrewd and even prophetic. "Such a man has a double existence: he may suffer misery, and be overwhelmed by disappointments, ... yet when he has retired into himself, he will be like a celestial spirit...."

In the last of Walton's introductory letters, dated August 19th, Victor admits that he has suffered grave consequences in his pursuit of knowledge and wisdom, and expresses a wish that Walton will not meet the same fate. "You seek for knowledge and wisdom, as I once did, and I ardently hope that the gratification of your wishes may not be a serpent to sting you, as mine has been." Walton is eager to hear his story, partly from curiosity and partly from a desire to alleviate Victor's suffering. While Victor thanks him for his concern, he also informs Walton that it is hopeless. The letter concludes with Victor promising to tell his tale the next day when he is "at leisure," and Walton resolving to record his tale each night, so that that he may preserve it for a future day.

Victor Frankenstein's Story

Chapter I begins with Victor Frankenstein narrating his family history and the story of his childhood to Robert Walton, aboard whose vessel he is now living. Born into a prestigious Genevese family, Victor's father, Alphonse Frankenstein, was married late in life following a career of public service. Having established his father's exemplary credentials, Victor then goes into considerable detail regarding the circumstances surrounding Alphonse Frankenstein's marriage to Caroline Beaufort. Caroline's father, referred to as Beaufort, was at one time an intimate friend of Alphonse Frankenstein. Beaufort fell into dire financial straits and, consequently, decided to leave town with his daughter, Caroline, in an effort to avoid humiliation. Alphonse, grieving for the absence of his trusted friend, finally located Beaufort and offered to help him, though the proud Beaufort turned him down. Beaufort eventually died of grief and his daughter, Caroline, was left an impoverished orphan. Alphonse, as her protector, left her in the care of a relative. Two years hence, in the first of many strange relationships in the Frankenstein household, Alphonse decided to marry Caroline. Indeed, a great deal of critical attention has been given to the strange formation of the Frankenstein household. Caroline Beaufort was at one time a "daughter" and then a wife to Alphonse, while Elizabeth Lavenza, whom we meet a little further on, is both Victor's "sister" and later his wife. With the subsequent birth of Victor and his other sons, Alphonse relinquished his life of public service so that he could devote his time to the education of his children. Though happily married, Caroline still longed to have a daughter and, by a strange quirk of fate, her wish was fulfilled. As it turned out, Alphonse's sister died and his brother-in-law, who planned on remarrying, requested that the Frankensteins assume responsibility for their niece, Elizabeth Lavenza. As to this last fact, we are told that Caroline and Alphonse were both determined from the outset that Victor marry Elizabeth as a means of solidifying the familial bond.

Victor portrays his childhood as one of perfect bliss, where peace and harmony prevail. In addition to Elizabeth, we are introduced to his cherished friend, Henry Clerval. Clerval is a sweet and creative boy, enamored of the tales of chivalry and romance from which he composes plays that he and Victor act out. As to their education at home, we are told that they were never forced to follow a strict regimen but, rather, were shown a purpose to their studies that in turn became a source of inspiration. However, into his portrait of an idyllic childhood, a sinister note is introduced when Victor tells us of his obsession with the works of Cornelius Agrippa (1486–1535), a reputed magician concerned with the occult and supernatural; Albertus Magnus (1234–1314), a German philosopher; and

Paracelsus (1493–1541), a Swiss physician who wrote works on alchemy,[1] chemistry, and medicine. As a result of his readings on the occult, Victor became preoccupied with discovering the philosopher's stone and the elixir of life. Victor became enthralled with a passion for probing the secrets of nature. To further augment his overzealousness, Victor reports how, at the age of about fifteen, he witnessed a bolt of lightning destroy a beautiful oak tree, turning it into a "blasted stump." "The catastrophe of this tree excited my extreme astonishment; and I eagerly inquired of my father the nature and origin of thunder and lightning." From that point on, Victor states that he rejected these same occult studies and instead became interested in natural philosophy. This new interest soon turned to disgust due to its new and incomprehensible vocabulary of chemical terms. The chapter concludes with Victor mentioning that he assumed responsibility for teaching his younger brother, Ernest, who had been ill since birth and thus lacked the stamina for rigorous study. He also makes a passing mention of his youngest brother, William, who at that time was an infant.

Victor relates that upon turning seventeen, his parents expected him to study at the University of Ingolstadt[2] (**Chapter II**). However, his departure was delayed when Elizabeth fell ill with scarlet fever. Though Elizabeth recovered, the incident led to his mother's tragic death. Longing to see Elizabeth, Caroline attended her daughter and became fatally ill as a consequence, leaving Elizabeth in charge of the younger Frankenstein children. More significantly, Caroline once again reiterates her wish that Elizabeth and Victor marry one day and exacted this deathbed promise from them. Victor describes how mourning for his mother turned to reflection on the evil reality of death, a thought that further provoked his overzealous pursuit to find a means to reverse human mortality. While the family coped with their loss, and Elizabeth attempted to revive the spirits of their aggrieved household, Victor prepared to leave for Ingolstadt, a departure marked by sadness. Accordingly, Victor arrived at Ingolstadt with a great deal of ambivalence. Though he felt lonely leaving his friends behind, he immediately became immersed in his scientific studies. At the university, he met Professor M. Krempe, whom he found rude, but knowledgeable. Krempe was contemptuous of the ancient authors Victor had read, declaring them to be ridiculous, "as musty as they are ancient," and insisting that Victor instead study the modern natural philosophers. But Victor was alienated by M. Krempe's attitude and, consequently, was disinclined to read the books he prescribed, finding that Krempe had merely cast aspersions on the writers who had inspired his current enthusiasm. "I was required to exchange chimeras of boundless grandeur for realities of little worth." However, Victor soon meets Professor M. Waldman, a teacher who stood in stark contrast to the detestable Krempe, and took an immediate liking to Waldman's kind disposition. Most appealing to Victor, however, was Waldman's enthusiasm for the modern philosophers who delved "into the recesses of nature, and [showed] how she works in her hiding places." Waldman praises the modern scientists whose works can "even mock the invisible world with its own shadows," a perspective that Victor found alluring. When Victor subsequently visited Waldman following a lecture, he expressed interest in becoming one of his disciples. Waldman showed him his laboratory with its various machines and promised to give Victor access once he advanced far enough in his studies "so as not to derange their mechanism." The chapter ends with Victor proclaiming that his destiny had now been decided.

With Waldman's help and encouragement, Victor vigorously renewed his study of chemistry and natural philosophy, forfeiting sleep while he read the prescribed works, and became increasingly preoccupied to the point that he lost all sense of time (**Chapter III**). Indeed, two years passed in the laboratory as Victor abandoned all thought of his family and friends. He was now isolated in his relentless pursuit of the principle of life, and completely immersed in the study of physiology and the structure of the human frame. When he finally began to think of his family back home, an incident took place that further distracted him from reestablishing human ties, namely, his ability to make improvements to some of the instruments in the laboratory, which in turn brought him prestige at the university. Following this, Victor became determined to wrest the secret of immortality by close observation of "the natural decay and corruption of the human body." His obsession took an even more sinister direction when he began to "spend days and nights in vaults and charnel houses," studying the minute details and changes that accompany death, a lurid task reminiscent of the gothic novels so popular in the latter part of the eighteenth century. These speculations took on an extreme hubris when Victor became convinced that despite all the brilliant scientists who preceded him, it would be his task alone to discover the cause of generation, making him "capable of bestowing animation upon lifeless matter." Yet now, in retrospect, he adds a caveat for Walton's benefit that such hubris will lead to irremediable consequences. Victor relates how he planned the next fateful step of fashioning an actual human being, someone about eight feet in height and proportionately large. In so doing, Victor became a supreme narcissist, poised to usurp divine authority and exhibiting all the false bravado that accompanies such claims to power. "Life and death appeared to me ideal bounds, which I should first break through, and pour a torrent of light into our dark world." Thus, he began to create a human being in "his workshop of filthy creation." Indeed, when Victor tells us that he was enslaved by his efforts in the laboratory, it is an ominous observation of the irrevocable change he has wrought in his own life, though he certainly did not realize this at this time.

Chapter IV of Victor's story describes a dreary and disquieting night in November as he contemplated infusing life into the creature. After years of relentless pursuit and study, he was filled with fear and trepidation with what he was about to do, and proceeded to infuse a spark of life which, though "successful," left him with a feeling of disgust. "I saw the dull yellow eye of the creature open; it breathed hard, and a convulsive motion agitated its limbs." Lamenting the catastrophic transformation of his dream into a nightmare as he gazed upon his horrid creation, Victor fled the laboratory, abandoning the creature at the hour of its birth. In so doing, Victor condemned both the monster and himself to a tortured existence that would become progressively worse with each passing day, a never-ending agony that would ultimately conclude in their mutual destruction. Though he ran away from the creature, Victor could find no reprieve from his guilt and anxiety. In fact, on this very same night, he tells Walton, he had a terrible nightmare in which he saw Elizabeth walking the streets of Ingolstadt only to discover that she was a ghost, resembling his mother. Meanwhile, the creature entered Victor's room in an attempt to speak to him, but Victor rushed out, fleeing "the demoniacal corpse to which [he] had so miserably given life." The next morning, Victor found that the gloomy weather mirrored his own despair. Nevertheless, he managed to find some solace when his dear friend, Henry Clerval, arrived in Ingolstadt. (Henry was finally able to convince his father to let him study at Ingolstadt, and had come to study foreign and ancient languages.) Victor then brought Henry to his living quarters, albeit fearfully, as he was dreading the appearance of the "monster." "I was unable to remain for a single instant in the same place; I jumped over the chairs, clapped my hands, and laughed aloud." Henry noticed Victor's strange behavior and thought he was sick. For his part, Victor soon succumbed to a nervous fever that lasted for several months, most especially because he could not divulge the terrible secret of what he had done. True to his loving character, Henry ministered to Victor while the latter, having finally regained his composure, declared himself ready to communicate with his family.

Chapter V begins with a description of a poignant letter he received from Elizabeth in which she described the family's concern about his recent illness. Though Victor's father had wanted to pay him a visit at Ingolstadt, Elizabeth was instrumental in stopping him. She relayed news of the rest of their family, describing how Ernest had grown up to be a healthy and active young man. Elizabeth also told him that Justine Moritz had returned to the Frankenstein household. Justine Moritz was a young girl who had been badly treated by her own mother and was later adopted by Victor's mother, Caroline, to whom she became very attached.

However, Justine, a devout Catholic, felt compelled to attend her own mother when she fell ill. Now that her own mother passed away, Justine returned to live with the Frankensteins. In response, Victor wrote back immediately to his family, but was easily fatigued from his long illness. Nevertheless, because his health was improving, he decided to show Henry around the university. However, Henry observed that the sight of laboratory instruments was loathsome for Victor, and quickly removed them. Professor Waldman, though, could not be avoided, and when he met the two friends, he began praising Victor's amazing accomplishments, whereupon he observed his student's discomfort and then launched into a discussion about science itself. Nevertheless, despite Waldman's attempt to be sensitive to his student's feelings, Victor found this alternative topic of conversation to be just as agonizing as the sight of laboratory instruments. Henry, ever sensitive to Victor's feelings, excused himself and gently changed the topic. When the two young men next encountered M. Krempe, the experience was even more painful to Victor. "M. Krempe was not equally docile; and in my condition at that time, of almost insupportable sensitiveness, his harsh blunt encomiums gave me even more pain...." All of the above notwithstanding, the chapter concludes with the summer months having brought some measure of rejuvenation for Victor and Clerval.

Chapter VI begins with Victor describing the letter he received from his father informing him that his younger brother, William, has been murdered, and the details of that heinous crime. Apparently, Alphonse, Elizabeth, William, and Ernest had gone for a walk in Plainpalais, when William suddenly got lost. When his lifeless body was discovered the following morning, it was presumed he was the victim of strangulation, the murderer's imprint having been found on his neck. Furthermore, a crucial piece of circumstantial evidence was discovered, namely, that a miniature portrait of Caroline that William had been wearing around his neck was now missing. Elizabeth apparently held herself responsible for William's death because she had given him the miniature, which the murderer was presumably willing to kill for.

Following this tragic event, Victor's father implored him to return home as soon as possible in order to help the family heal. Thus, Victor embarked upon a "melancholy journey" back to Geneva. Along the way, he observed familiar scenes that now caused him unbearable pain, and experienced vague intimations of impending horrors. "One sudden and desolate change had taken place; ... I dared not advance, dreading a thousand nameless evils that made me tremble, although I was unable to define them." Accordingly, Victor remained at Lausanne for two days and managed to regain some degree of equilibrium, though he was flooded with feelings of grief as he approached Geneva. It was now dark and the town gates of Geneva had been shut, causing him to spend the night in the village of Secheron, where he decided to visit the spot where William was murdered. However, in order to do so, he first had to cross a lake, during a storm, in order to get to Plainpalais, the scene of the crime. Indeed, the weather seemed to be in sync with his inner torment. The scene was sublime[3] in the true romantic sense, eliciting awesome yet terrifying beauty as a sudden burst of lightning reveals the "filthy daemon" lurking in the shadows. Victor immediately understood that William's murderer was none other than his monster, though pursuing this wily creature during a storm would be futile. In this brief instant Victor was also reminded of his own evil nature. "I considered the being whom I had cast among mankind.... nearly in the light of my own vampire, my own spirit let loose from the grave, and forced to destroy all that was dear to me." Victor likewise realized that the people around him would never believe his seemingly preposterous story. When he finally reached home, Ernest told him that Justine Moritz was believed to be the murderer, as the miniature was found in the pocket of her dress, linking her to an obvious motive. Victor was shocked and protested her innocence, because he alone knew with certainty that Justine had been framed. Tragically, in the interim, the incriminating circumstantial evidence continued to mount against her. In addition to her exhibiting very confused behavior following the murder, one of the servants had testified that she found Justine in possession of the miniature. However, most significantly and above all other appalling circumstances was the fact that although Victor knew the monster to be the true culprit, he was enjoined from speaking on Justine's behalf because to do so would reveal his unspeakable secret. Nevertheless, Victor refused to believe that Justine would be unjustly convicted of murder, and repeatedly assured the family that she would be acquitted. "I had no fear, therefore, that any circumstantial evidence could be brought forward strong enough to convict her; and, in this assurance, I calmed myself, expecting the trial with eagerness, but without prognosticating an evil result."

In **Chapter VII,** Victor describes the Frankenstein family's attendance at Justine's trial, as witnesses, as Victor's self-assurance eroded with his increasing and unbearable inner turmoil. "During the whole of this wretched mockery of justice, I suffered living torture." It is important to note that Victor's claim that he would have testified on her behalf but for the fact that he was far from home at the time of the murder and thus lacked credibility as a witness, is deceptive; not only did he know the monster to be the true culprit, he was also painfully aware that his testimony would have necessitated the exposure of his hideous creation. In the absence of Victor's crucial testimony, the circumstantial evidence remained incriminating, especially when it was revealed that Justine was not home on the night of the murder. To add to Justine's presumed guilt, a market-woman testified that she saw her the next morning in the very same place where William's corpse was discovered. Moreover, when Justine returned home on the night of the murder, she became hysterical and confined herself to her bed upon seeing the corpse. It was then that the servant found the miniature in her dress. When Justine finally testified in her own defense, her simple and honest statements were unavailing. The truth is that she had passed the evening at her aunt's home in Chêne and, upon returning home around nine o'clock, met a man who inquired about the lost child, at which point she became alarmed and decided to look for William herself. However, because the gates of the town had already been closed, she was forced to spend a sleepless night outside the town, during which she resumed her search for William. Justine also stated truthfully that she had no idea why the miniature was found in her possession, her bewilderment only adding to her appearance of guilt. Though other witnesses knew her fine character, the hideous nature of the crime rendered them unable to speak on her behalf. Elizabeth Lavenza, however, was shocked by their cowardice and countered their silence by attesting to Justine's virtuous nature. But, alas, Justine is condemned to death and finally "admits" to the crime, though sadly no one, including Elizabeth, realized her admission was made under extreme pressure by her confessor. When Elizabeth and Victor subsequently visited Justine in prison, she protested her innocence, explaining that if she had not confessed she would have faced excommunication. Justine ultimately dies a condemned murderer. It is important to note that this entire trial, a complete travesty of justice, can also be read as Mary Shelley's critique of both the criminal justice system and institutionalized religion. As a result of these terrible events in the first part of his narrative, Victor represents himself to Walton as a man beyond all hope of salvation, condemned to live in a world reminiscent of Dante's *Inferno*. "Anguish and despair had penetrated into the core of my heart; I bore a hell within me, which nothing could extinguish."

VOLUME II
The Monster's Story
Chapter I begins with Victor Frankenstein's description of his own inner torment following Justine's execution, a psychic paralysis of "inaction and certainty" far beyond articulation, compounded by the ensuing misery it has brought upon Elizabeth. "'I was seized by a remorse and sense of guilt, which hurried me away to a hell of intense tortures, such as no language can describe.'" Not by coincidence, Victor is increasingly made to endure the same emotional pain and accompanying physical distress inflicted upon his despised creature; his only relief is isolation. "[S]olitude was my only consolation—deep, dark, death-like solitude." Furthermore, similar to what the monster will soon relate concerning his

initial intentions, Victor is forced to reflect upon the extent of his own fall from a benevolent being who sought to help mankind to a tormented soul with no means of escape, an obvious allusion to the Satan of *Paradise Lost*. His father, however, mistakes his wish to be alone as excessive sorrow at William's death, and decides that a change in atmosphere would be best for the whole family. Thus, the move to Belrive brings an anticipated benefit from Victor's perspective as he has felt like a prisoner when the gates of their Geneva house are shut by ten o'clock every night. Victor tells us that he was in the habit of sailing on the lake for hours, oftentimes forced to spend the night on the water, alone with his own "miserable reflections." Indeed, by the beginning of Volume II, he has become so utterly hopeless that he even contemplates suicide by "plunging into the silent lake," but for the fact that it would leave his already distressed family vulnerable to the violence of his sworn enemy. In truth, as we will be continually reminded throughout his narrative, there is absolutely no means of escape from his predicament, only a few fleeting instances in which he is sufficiently distracted. As proof of his inescapability, Victor has by now begun to anticipate future destruction and mayhem from his creature and, consequently, acquires an obsessive desire and firm resolution to take revenge. It is now August, nearly two months since Justine's execution, when Victor decides to make an excursion (a term that in itself means a turning away from a given course), with Elizabeth and Ernest, to the valley of Chamouni in yet another doomed attempt to run way from himself and his monstrous creation. With its sublime and other-earthly landscape of great snowy mountains and glaciers, Chamouni offers only a temporary reprieve as we are told in the beginning of **Chapter II**. "They elevated me from all littleness of feeling; and although they did not remove my grief, they subdued and tranquillized it." It is now the second day, and the weather is fair as Victor and his siblings continue along their excursion.

The following morning, however, is rainy and foggy, obscuring the view of the Alps. Victor's melancholy has now returned as he wishes to regain enough self-composure so that he may conceal his true feelings. It is now apparent that this is the most he can hope for. Despite the inclement weather, Victor goes off alone to the summit of Montanvert where he gazes upon a huge and continually moving glacier, a view that fills him with a "sublime ecstasy that gave wings to the soul." Nevertheless, as we have come to expect, Victor enjoys a mere few moments before his joy reverts to horror when he discerns the figure of a man moving across the ice at superhuman speed, a being of "unearthly ugliness," his hideous daemon. Indeed, Victor becomes so enraged that he barely notices the monster's anguished facial expression, a symptomatic shortsightedness that plagues him throughout the novel for, had he truly looked at his monster from the outset rather than running away in fear, he might have given the creature a "sympathetic eye" and treated him accordingly. Instead Victor now calls his monster a devil while the monster, to its credit, appears eminently reasonable in response. In a calm manner, he asks Victor to simply honor the responsibility he has toward his creation and remains steadfast while pleading with Victor to fashion him a suitable female companion. "Do your duty towards me, and I will do mine towards you and the rest of mankind." At this juncture, the monster clearly has the upper hand given the superior language skills he has acquired during his exile, while Victor increasingly experiences an inability to articulate his thoughts. Indeed, the monster proves to be a consummate rhetorician, pleading his cause with a "father" who has thus far refused to respond to his child's plea for justice. The monster sees himself in a Miltonic context, claiming that he has been forced to hate his "creator," just as Lucifer had turned against God. "Remember, that I am thy creature. I ought to be thy Adam, but I am rather the fallen angel, whom thou drivest from joy for no misdeed." That the monster has at least succeeded in getting his attention is manifested by Victor's statement that he "weighed the various arguments that he had used" and determined to at least listen. While the monster narrates his tale, Victor is anxious to determine whether or not he killed William and then framed Justine.

The monster tells Victor that, since leaving Ingolstadt, he has been forced to wander in the neighboring woods while attempting to become acclimated to his senses. Indeed, as the monster's story unfolds it is the description of a quasi-evolution taking us through his strange birth and infancy to a surprising level of maturity. The monster has been and will forever remain a strange being who has been left completely to his own devices and, having been neither nurtured nor schooled, has been compelled to act as his own parent at the same time (**Chapter III**). Before leaving Victor's apartment, the monster felt cold and covered himself with some clothes, but these proved insufficient. After several days of alternating sun and darkness, the monster began to commune with nature, enjoying many new and pleasant sounds when, fortuitously, he discovered a warm fire and the materials by which it can be made. However, food was becoming scarce as his supply of berries and nuts was dwindling and the monster had to endure hunger. Fortunately, he discovered a shepherd's hut in the woods and examined it with great curiosity as it is a structure that afforded protection from the elements, as well as a ready supply of food. "[I]t presented to me then as exquisite and divine a retreat as Pandemonium appeared to the daemons of hell after their sufferings in the lake of fire." What is most striking about this description is that during his interval in the forest, he has acquired an amazing degree of literacy displayed here in his allusion to Book I of *Paradise Lost*.

Having left the hut, the monster then walked until he reached a village of attractive homes and cottages, and settled into a vacant yet comfortable structure, making it even more habitable by carpeting it with clean straw, "a paradise, compared to the bleak forest." From this vantage point, the monster describes his observations of the hardworking De Lacey family. Through a chink in a boarded-up window, the monster became intent on observing this family, both the young people and the old man and, in so doing, reveals himself ˹˗ ˺ be a creature of keen sensitivity to the feelings of others.

ver hair and benevolent countenance of the aged
, won my reverence; while the gentle manners of the

girl enticed my love." As night falls, **Chapter III** concludes with the monster perceiving an inexplicable communication taking place between the young man and his elder. "[T]he youth began, not to play [on an instrument], but to utter sounds that were monotonous, and neither resembling the harmony of the old man's instrument or the song of birds. I since found that he read aloud, but at that time I knew nothing of the science of words or letters."

Chapter IV continues with the monster telling Victor about his self-education through his rapt attention to the De Lacey family. Indeed, so keen is the monster's attention to all aspects of the De Lacey family that he even discerns an air of unhappiness in their household as a result of their poverty. In yet another demonstration of loving kindness, the monster states that although he was previously wont to steal food from them at night, his newfound awareness of their own privation moved him to forage for food of his own and to collect wood at night for the benefit of the De Lacey family. The monster had become enchanted with these "lovely creatures" and soon discovered, from a distance, what he discerned to be language as the medium of their communication. "I perceived that the words they spoke sometimes produced pleasure or pain, smiles or sadness, in the minds and countenances of the hearers.... This was indeed a godlike science, and I ardently desired to become acquainted with it." He also learns their names—*Agatha* or *sister* and *Felix* or *son*. The monster spends the winter in this manner, sympathizing alike with the De Laceys in their joys and sorrows, and developing a profound appreciation for their ability to find happiness in the simplest of things, despite their poverty. As he further relates to Victor, the monster also began to learn the fundamentals of reading by listening as Felix read to his father and sister. Above all else, however, the monster had an ardent desire to make his presence known to the family and thereby become a part of their domestic circle, which he hoped to accomplish through a "gentle demeanour and conciliating words." This statement is significant because it is a strategy necessitated by the monster's awareness of his hideous appearance. As he tells Victor, he saw his own reflection in a pool, yet despite his feelings of self-revulsion, his desire for a family was stronger. Furthermore, the advent of spring and the cheerful aspect of nature providing further inducements, the monster then resolved that he would eventually introduce himself to the De Laceys. "My spirits were elevated by the enchanting appearance of nature; the past was blotted from my memory, the present was tranquil, and the future gilded by bright rays of hope, and the anticipations of joy."

In **Chapter V**, the monster exhibits an urgency to get to the more "moving" part of his story and those observations that made a profound impression on him. The inaugural event was the arrival of a visitor on horseback, a strange lady with raven black hair and angelic features, who came to see Felix. The mysterious lady is Safie, a beautiful Arabian woman, with whom Felix appeared to be in love as his face lit up upon seeing her. The monster also observes that the young woman speaks a different language than the De Laceys and that she was endeavoring to learn their language by repeating various sounds, concluding that he too can learn by her example. Furthermore, the monster was also learning to read what Safie was being taught. " 'While I improved in speech, I also learned the science of letters, as it was taught to the stranger.' " From Volney's *Ruins of Empires* (1791), he learned "the manners, governments, and religions of the different nations of the earth" and gained an insight into the abuse of political power and the resulting destruction of people and culture. This newly acquired knowledge then led to further depressing thoughts as the monster began to ponder his own displaced status. "Was I then a monster, a blot upon the earth, from which all men fled, and whom all disowned?" Clearly, his idyllic sojourn in the forest began to fall apart as he continued to learn the truth about human nature and to understand that he can never hope to be a part of it. "Was man, indeed, at once so powerful, so virtuous, and magnificent, yet so vicious and base?" As a result of his ennobling education and scrutiny of the loving De Lacey family, the monster's bitterness was heightened, and will continue to be inflamed, because he is to be permanently excluded from the gifts of social contact and communion. "But where were my friends and relations? No father had watched my infant days, no mother had blessed me with smiles and caresses." Alas, knowledge had brought further despondency over his own alienated and revolting existence.

In **Chapter VI**, the monster continues to tell Victor about the De Lacey family history. Apparently, the old man, referred to as simply De Lacey, came from a prominent family in France, participating in all matters of culture and intellect. His son, Felix, was raised to serve his country, while his daughter, Agatha, acquired the status of a well-bred lady. They had previously lived a luxurious life in Paris, and were immersed in all matters of culture and intellect. It was Safie's father, a Turkish merchant, who was the cause of their ruin and, indirectly, the reason for Felix having made Safie's acquaintance. For some unexplained reason, her father had offended the authorities and was eventually condemned to death. However, it was generally believed that he was the victim of religious and economic prejudice, having been a wealthy foreigner. Felix, who had been present at the trial, was enraged by the whole affair and decided to help Safie's father to escape from prison. Though her father offered Felix wealth and reward in exchange for his help, this offer is later revealed to be a ruse. Perceiving that Felix had fallen in love with Safie, her father promises her hand in marriage. True to his character, Felix, who was too sensitive to accept the offer, nevertheless was hopeful that, in time, he would in fact be with Safie. During this interval while her father's escape was being planned, Safie had written to Felix explaining that her mother was a Christian Arab who had been enslaved by the Turks until Safie's father married her.

On the day preceding the planned execution, however, Felix helped the condemned man to escape to some undisclosed place in Paris and even obtained passports for himself, Agatha, and their father, giving them safe passage through to Leghorn, where her father intended to find a way back to Turkey. Felix was not aware of the merchant's ultimate agenda, which was to take Safie back with him to Constantinople, having never really considered Felix, a Christian, to be a suitable husband. Felix was simply a means to flee France. In the meantime, the French government was enraged by the escape and was determined to punish the Turk's deliverer. The entire plot being soon discovered, Agatha and her father, De Lacey, were imprisoned, since Felix was living with Safie and her father. When Felix heard about what happened to his family, he resolved to deliver himself to the law in exchange for their release but, alas, they remained imprisoned for five months prior to their trial and, as a result of that trial, lost their fortune and were exiled from France. Agatha and De Lacey eventually took up residence in a cottage in Germany, which is where the monster discovered them. In the meantime, Felix soon discovers the duplicity of the Turkish merchant who, upon learning of the suffering that the De Laceys now endured, made a very offensive gesture by offering a paltry sum of money, at the same time that he kept his daughter with him. Nevertheless, Safie remained steadfast in her wish to be with Felix and after learning of Felix's whereabouts, set out for Germany in the company of a female attendant. During the journey the attendant became very sick and consequently died, but not before instructing their hostess regarding their final destination. Thus, Safie was on her own when she arrived safely at the De Lacey cottage.

Nevertheless, the story of deception and unfaithfulness notwithstanding, the monster is still in the process of learning his true standing in the human community and reiterates his desire to become a viable member of society (**Chapter VII**). In his own words, he deems the tragic De Lacey history to be "a distant evil; [because] benevolence and generosity were ever present before me, inciting within me a desire to become an actor in the busy scene where so many admirable qualities were called forth and displayed." At this juncture, the monster still believed that he would be able to ingratiate himself with the De Lacey family.

The monster also tells Victor that he discovered a leather portmanteau, which contained clothing and several classic books, among them *Paradise Lost*, which filled him with awe and an image of an omnipotent God at war with his creation; *Plutarch's Lives*, from which he has read the account of ancient republics and the lofty thoughts of its leaders and heroes; and *The Sorrows of Young Werther*, where he read of the same tender domesticity that he observed in the De Laceys and developed an admiration for Werther, an unpretentious young man whose disquisitions on suicide elicited great sympathy.

We also learn that the monster had stolen some papers from Victor's laboratory which recorded Victor's thoughts and actions for four months preceding the creation of his monster. These papers also documented Victor's feelings of revulsion once his experiment was brought to completion. Sickened by what he read, the monster accuses Victor of consigning his creature to a life of despondency and solitude. "God in pity made man beautiful and alluring, after his own image, but my form is a filthy type of yours, more horrid from its very resemblance." With this searing indictment, the monster judges Victor guilty for usurping God's authority simply for his own selfish reasons. He further states to Victor that he considers himself to be another manifestation of Victor Frankenstein. Nevertheless, the monster had not yet tested his ability to find friendship and compassion in other human beings and, thus, was still hopeful despite his newly acquired knowledge of his creator. Lonely and desperate, the monster observed the joy that Safie infused into the De Lacey household and, thus, decided to seek their protection. His plan was to begin by approaching the old man when the others were out.

During this time, the monster tells of his experiencing the change of seasons from spring into fall and the accompanying decay of nature, stating that he is constitutionally suited to the ensuing cold, though his true source of delight is with the warmth and colors of summer. It was autumn when the monster finally mustered the courage to speak to the blind old man, introducing himself as a weary traveler in need of rest. When the old man asked him if he was a Frenchman, the monster cleverly replied that he had been educated by a French family, and then quickly changed the subject to his need for companionship, "an unfortunate and deserted creature" who sought protection from this yet-to-be-identified family, but whom he feared will be prejudiced against him. Winning the old man's sympathy by appealing to his benevolence and his experience of betrayal, the monster finally revealed that it was the De Lacey family whom he desired to be friends with. At the very moment of this startling revelation, Felix, Safie, and Agatha entered the cottage and were astounded at the sight of the monster. "Who can describe their horror and consternation on beholding me?" In response, Safie rushed out of the cottage, Agatha fainted, and Felix snatched his father away while viciously beating the monster with a stick. With this new demonstration of man's cruelty, the monster escaped to his cottage filled with pain and bitterness.

Chapter VIII begins with the monster cursing his plight after this latest cruelty at the hands of people he had learned to love. Leaving his cottage at night, he began to wander, railing against his mean existence. "I, like the arch fiend, bore a hell within me; and finding myself unsympathized with, wished to tear up the trees, spread havoc, and destruction around me, and then to have sat down and enjoyed the ruin." The next morning, feeling restored by the sunshine, the monster heard some men close by and realized that he must remain in the forest, avoiding detection. During this interval, he had a chance to reflect on the events of the prior day and decided that his plan failed because it was imprudent to reveal himself to the children where he should have taken the old man into his confidence first. Thus, the monster concluded that he would try once again to speak to De Lacey and "by my representations win him to my pity." But, alas, this new plan is doomed. As the monster approaches the De Lacey residence, he hears Felix speaking with his landlord and learns that the family is leaving because they fear for the life of the father. Filled with hopelessness and an inconsolable sense of loss, the monster's anguish turned to feelings of revenge as he resolved to set fire to the cottage. "My protectors had departed, and had broken the only link that held me to the world.... I bent my mind towards injury and death." Having destroyed all vestiges of the De Laceys, the monster headed toward Geneva to seek out his creator and find some relief from his dire circumstances. During his nighttime travels, the monster endured cold once again, all the while feelings of revenge were welling up inside him. When he finally reached Switzerland, he found the sun to be warmer and he used the daylight hours to rest, finding some measure of gentleness and tranquillity. While enjoying these feelings of restoration, he came across a young girl who slipped and fell into a rapid stream, and succeeded in saving her life. But, alas, her guardian, terrified to see her with this hideous creature, shot and wounded the monster. "This was then the reward of my benevolence!" The monster thus remained in the woods for a few weeks so that his wound could heal.

Upon reaching Geneva, the monster relates how he met a beautiful and innocent child whom he wanted to educate and keep as his own. However, upon learning that the child was a member of the Frankenstein family, he instead strangled the child, exclaiming that "I, too, can create desolation." Furthermore, in yet another gesture of revenge, the monster describes how he took the miniature of the beautiful lady from the child's breast and planted it in Justine's dress, whom he found sleeping nearby. Thus, Victor receives confirmation of his brother's murderer and the monster's vicious framing of Justine for this heinous crime. The monster is clearly determined to visit the same injustice to which he has been condemned upon Victor and all those he loves. Following his spate of murder and pillage, the monster is now firmly resolved that Victor must create another creature with the very same defects, a female, to keep him company.

In **Chapter IX**, the monster completes his tale and demands that Victor comply with his request for a companion. For his part, Victor is angered at all that has transpired and at first refuses to submit to the monster's mandate. "Shall I create another like yourself, whose joint wickedness might desolate the world. Begone!" Swearing unremitting hatred, the monster is quick to point out that Victor is not only responsible for bringing this loveless and unloved creature into the world, he is obligated to provide him with a companion. "Oh! my creator, make me happy; let me feel gratitude towards you for one benefit." In the face of this irrefutable argument, Victor is moved. "His tale, and the feelings he now expressed, proved him to be a creature of fine sensations." Moreover, as a further inducement to comply with his request, the creature promises to stay as far away as possible from humankind. "My evil passions will have fled me, for I shall meet with sympathy; my life will flow quietly away, and, in my dying moments, I shall not curse my maker." With Victor consenting to his final demand, conditioned on the premise that the creature leave Europe forever, the creature agrees never to visit Frankenstein again once his companion is delivered. But this promise takes its toll on Victor, leaving him with a heavy heart. When he gets back to Chamouni the following day, his family is alarmed to see him so distressed and they immediately return to their home in Geneva while Victor seemingly regains some composure as he falls into the routine of everyday life.

VOLUME III
Victor Pursues His Monster

Though the duality of characterization must be assumed from the beginning, in this last volume Victor and his monster, creator and daemon, are inextricably intertwined in thought and deed. They are enslaved by each other. Unable to fashion a suitable female companion for fear of creating another being capable of wreaking further chaos, Victor reneges on his commitment. However, his monster has been vigilantly tracking Victor's "progress" and has promised disastrous consequences should his demands not be met.

Chapter I begins with Victor describing his ambivalence. While he was afraid of disappointing the monster, he was deeply concerned about unleashing a second creature. "I feared the vengeance of the disappointed fiend, yet I was unable to overcome my repugnance to the task which was enjoined me." As a result of his inner conflict, Victor procrastinated as much as possible, finding solace in solitude. His father, noticing his erratic emotions, reminded him of yet another commitment, namely, that he was expected to marry Elizabeth as a way of assuring domestic harmony in the Frankenstein family. Victor assured his father that this would come to pass, but expressed a wish to tour the continent for the next two years with his dear friend, Henry Clerval, before settling down. Both Elizabeth and his father consented to the delay, having absolutely no clue regarding Victor's secret agenda. For that matter, neither did Henry Clerval. With this pretext, a very apprehensive Victor Frankenstein traveled to London where he hoped to learn about the discoveries of an English philosopher that he hoped would prove useful to his task, all the while thinking about the monster's promise to watch his every move. As it was August and the time of vintage, Victor and Clerval enjoyed the magnificent scenery as they traveled along the Rhine. Once they arrived in London, however, Clerval was anxious to speak with the "men of genius and talent who flourished at the time," while Victor was preoccupied with getting access to the information necessary for constructing his new creature (**Chapter II**). It was now October and Victor's state of mind was extremely agitated, and Clerval's presence served as a painful reminder of happier days before he hatched his disastrous experiment. "[A] blight had overcome my existence, and I only visited these people for the sake of the information they might give me on the subject in which my interest was so terribly profound." Some months later, after gathering the necessary chemical instruments and materials, Victor and Henry Clerval, at the invitation of a friend, departed for some isolated region in the highlands of Scotland. They left on March 27th and spent a few days at Windsor, followed by a visit to Oxford where they delighted in a countryside that was associated with so much of English history. Further on, their travels took them to Cumberland and Westmoreland, where they made some pleasant acquaintances, and then to the romantic town of Edinburgh. But these temporary diversions notwithstanding, Victor had become increasingly disturbed as he was reminded of his sinister mission. "But I am a blasted tree; ... a miserable spectacle of wrecked humanity, pitiable to others and abhorrent to myself."

As the two continued their travels through northern England where they were to meet their friend, Victor expressed a desire to visit Scotland alone, intending to find a desolate place in the northern highlands, a remote part of the world where there would be absolutely no distractions, though Henry tried to dissuade him. Victor eventually found such a place in "one of the remotest of the Orkneys as the scene of [his] labors," a place that mirrored his desperate solitude and utter hopelessness. There were but three "miserable" huts on the island, one of which was vacant. Victor rented it immediately to use as his laboratory and living quarters. The hut, consisting of two rooms, was in miserable condition, but after making some repairs and buying some furniture, Victor fell into a routine of working during the day and walking along the stony beach at night. While separated from all mankind in this forsaken land, Victor still experienced wild mood swings, sometimes finding it impossible to work "on this filthy process" and at other times compelled to work at a feverish pace. Ever mindful that the monster was watching and could appear at any moment, Victor was also plagued with serious misgivings about bringing his anticipated creature into being. Nevertheless, **Chapter II** concludes with Victor having made considerable progress.

Chapter III continues on a late evening while Victor, working in his laboratory, was thinking of the consequences of his current employment and the time that had elapsed since he created his first monster. Above all else, however, he thought anxiously about the possibility that his two creatures would be able to reproduce, giving birth to "a race of devils" that he feared "might make the very existence of the species of man a condition precarious and full of terror." As he meditated upon what he considered to be the monster's specious arguments, Victor imagined incurring the wrath of future generations for the sake of gaining his own peace of mind. At this very moment, the monster appeared with an extremely menacing expression, while Victor, in a panic, destroyed his nearly completed creation. "[T]rembling with passion, [I] tore to pieces the thing on which I was engaged." Vowing never to resume his labors, Victor fled the laboratory and locked the door. Several hours passed as he gazed out at the motionless sea when, suddenly, the monster reappeared and confronted him, demanding to know Victor's intentions now that he had destroyed the monster's last hope. Though Victor ordered him to leave, he commanded in vain. In response, the monster stated very clearly that despite the reasonableness of his entreaties, Victor had recoiled from his ethical responsibility and, in that abnegation of that obligation, had indeed allowed the monster to gain ascendancy and moral authority over him. "Slave, I before reasoned with you, but you have proved yourself unworthy of my condescension." The monster declared that Victor would forever remain his captive and vowed to wreak his revenge. "You can blast my other passions; but revenge remains—revenge, henceforth dearer than light or food!" When Victor made one more futile attempt to order the monster out of his sight, the creature made one more ominous promise. "It is well, I go; but remember, I shall be with you on your wedding night." Having eluded Victor's grasp, the creature left immediately in his boat, moving rapidly through the water. His last chilling words, however, were branded onto Victor's brain. "In that hour I should die, and at once satisfy and extinguish his malice." Victor knew that his fate had been sealed, recognizing that only death could bring an end to his misery. His sole remaining fear was for those family members whom the monster had not yet destroyed.

Following the monster's departure, Victor contemplated his bleak alternatives. He could either remain in this barren terrain or return to his family and await the further sacrifice of his loved ones. While here, however, he fell asleep in the grass and, in a pattern familiar to both him and his monster, he awakened the next morning refreshed and happier despite the tormented feelings and violent happenings he experienced just a few hours earlier. A letter from Henry Clerval asking him to join him in Perth served to reinforce those feelings of well-being. But, before he could leave, Victor had to dispose of the body of the monster's companion, which he decided to dump into the sea late at night in a basket weighed down with stones. Once again, he was compelled to return to his laboratory and relive the horror he so desperately wanted to escape. It becomes Victor's return to his own peculiar "primal scene." "I must pack my chemical instruments; and for that purpose I must enter the room which had been the scene of my odious work, and I must handle those utensils, the sight of which was sickening to me." Upon completion of his task, Victor remained at sea a little while longer and fell asleep. When he wakened the next morning in his skiff, he found that he had been driven off course and was now totally lost. Hungry and fatigued, he found himself in a civilized yet hapless Irish town, which mirrored the experience of his monster who, coming in peace and friendship, instead became a pariah. Though at first Victor was relieved to find that the inhabitants spoke English, his hopes were quickly dashed when he was greeted rudely and told to appear before the magistrate, Mr. Kirwin. Victor then learned that a dead body had been found under suspicious circumstances and that he was expected to offer an explanation. Immediately despised by the locals whose "faces expressed a mixture of curiosity and hatred," the chapter ends ominously as Victor recalls "the frightful events" that he is about to describe to Walton.

Chapter IV opens with Victor's description of his appearance before the magistrate at which time he learned that a dead body had been found and that he was the suspect. As he listened to the details, Victor was suddenly seized with a familiar dread. The body they recovered was that of a handsome young man who showed signs of being strangled, bearing marks similar to the ones found on his brother William. It also turned out that the facts surrounding Victor's alleged guilt were circumstantial as they were in Justine's case. Incriminating evidence was offered through the testimony of Daniel Nugent, his son, and brother-in-law, who were out fishing when they stumbled upon a young man's body lying on the beach. The main witness gave further incriminating evidence, stating that he saw a single man out in a boat that night, while other village residents offered similar descriptions. Following this damning testimony, Victor was asked to view the dead body so that the magistrate could observe his reaction. The sight of the corpse filled Victor with horror when he recognized the corpse to be that of Henry Clerval. Filled with an inconsolable remorse, Victor had convulsions and was bedridden for over two months, during which time he raved that he was the murderer. When he awoke, Victor found himself in prison. Though he started to recover, it was only to be painfully aware of his wretched circumstances and, once again, he reflected that only death could release him from his predicament. Mr. Kirwin, however, proved himself a sympathetic magistrate, providing Victor with the best possible prison accommodations as well as a physician and a nurse to look after him. The benevolent Mr. Kirwin also contacted Victor's family and Alphonse Frankenstein came, though the visit with his son was brief due to the fact that Victor's health was still in a precarious state. Seeing his father did bring a modicum of relief until his thoughts returned to Clerval's murder. When court proceedings resumed, Victor was spared criminal charges and allowed to return home due to Kirwin's kindly intervention. Victor and Alphonse then set sail for Havre-de-Grâce. Though Victor was now taking laudanum at night in order to get some rest, the medication did not prevent a "kind-of nightmare" in which the monster appeared to hold Victor firmly in his clutches.

Chapter V begins with Victor describing how he and his father went to Havre, so as to avoid London and the memories of happier times that he and Henry Clerval shared. For his part, Alphonse's energies were wholly devoted to nurturing his son back to health and happiness. Despite Victor's claim of responsibility for the deaths of Justine, William, and Henry, Alphonse believed his son to be deranged. "[W]hen I thus accused myself, he sometimes seemed to desire an explanation, and at others he appeared to consider it as caused by delirium."

Before they left for Paris, Victor received a letter from Elizabeth, assuring him of her unfailing love and wanting his pledge that he was marrying her for love rather than from any sense of obligation. She had apparently mistaken Victor's need for solitude as a sign of his disinterest in her. This letter, of course, reminded Victor of the fiend's promise to interfere on his wedding day and, weighing the monster's threats against the joy his marriage would bring to both Elizabeth and his father, Victor resolved to go forward with the marriage. He wrote her a loving and reassuring letter, stating that he intended to explain all of his problems on the day they are married. "I will confide this tale of misery and terror to you the day after our marriage shall take place; for, my sweet cousin, there must be perfect confidence between us." Until then, he asked her to be patient.

When Victor returned home, he courted Elizabeth for a while, though his torment persisted. His father, however, was pressuring Victor to get married soon so that their loving circle would be complete, and Victor relented because he could not bear the thought of losing Elizabeth. Victor also foolishly believed that the monster's threat related only to himself and not to Elizabeth. As the time for the wedding drew near, Victor became extremely paranoid and, consequently, armed himself with many weapons. "I carried pistols and a dagger constantly about me, and was ever on the watch to prevent artifice; and by these means gained a greater degree of tranquility." After the wedding ceremony, Victor and Elizabeth left for Cologne, while Victor was well aware that these were the last days of happiness he would ever enjoy. Nevertheless, despite this happy occasion, Elizabeth had a vague premonition of impending evil, though she resisted giving in to it, but not so for Victor whose heart was heavy. "The sun sunk beneath the horizon as we landed; and as I touched the shore, I felt those cares and fears revive, which soon were to clasp me, and cling to me forever."

Chapter VI opens with Victor describing his arrival in Cologne. He and Elizabeth had walked along the shore for a while and then returned to the inn due to an impending storm. As it began to rain, Victor's terror intensified and he fully expected the monster to appear at any moment. He even left the room to check the surroundings before retiring when, all of a sudden, he heard shrill and dreadful screams from Elizabeth's room. Victor returned to find his bride dead, "lifeless and inanimate ... her pale and distorted features half covered by her hair." Immediately upon making this tragic discovery Victor again expressed his recurring wish to die. "Great God! Why did I not then expire." Following this anguished outcry, Victor fainted for a moment only to reawaken and find himself surrounded by a crowd of people from the inn looking on in shock. Their horrified expression serving as a painful mockery of his inner torment, Victor fled and rushed into the room where Elizabeth's body lay, embracing her lifeless form. "The murderous mark of the fiend's grasp on her neck, and the breath had ceased to issue from her lips." While still hovering over the body, Victor happened to look up at the window, and found the monster grinning at him against the nightmarish background of a pale moon. "The shutters had been thrown back; and with a sensation of horror not to be described, [Victor] saw at the open window a figure the most hideous and abhorred." Though he rushed at the fiend, Victor failed to shoot him and the monster was able to escape with the swiftness of lightning, plunging into the lake. A search party then formed and set out in a fruitless attempt to trap the culprit with Victor pointing them in the fiend's direction. After several hours they returned unsuccessful, whereupon they set out to search the forest, this time without Victor.

In the meantime, Victor, now alone in his room, began to think about the devastating effect this latest tragedy would have on his father and realized that his father and Ernest could become the next victims. "I was bewildered in a cloud of wonder and horror. The death of William, the execution of Justine, the murder of Clerval, and lastly my wife: even at that moment I knew not that my only remaining friends were safe from the malignity of the fiend." Horrified at this consideration, Victor left promptly for home. However, since there were no horses for hire, he had no alternative but to return by the lake—the same lake into which the fiend had previously escaped—during the early morning hours with an unfavorable wind and a torrent of rain hailing down. Though he had looked forward to physical exertion as a way to channel his mental torment, Victor found that his agitation had become so overwhelming as to render him powerless. Furthermore, the surrounding landscape underscored his pain by reminding him of happier days when Elizabeth was alive. "A fiend had snatched from me every hope of future happiness."

When he got back to Geneva, his father, the eternal optimist, was finally rendered inconsolable with grief over Elizabeth's death and died soon after in Victor's arms. "I see him now, excellent and venerable old man! his eyes wandered in vacancy, for they had lost their charm and their delight—his niece, his more than daughter.... Cursed, cursed be the fiend that brought misery on his grey hairs, and doomed him to waste in wretchedness." Naturally, these last two tragedies took their toll on Victor's mental health. Considered to be a madman, Victor was then put in solitary confinement for a while and, in a month's time following his release, he voluntarily appeared before a criminal judge for the purpose of identifying the real murderer and requesting help from the law. Though we are not given the precise details of the story he told to the judge, it is significant that Victor was finally able to articulate his strange tale, indicating that he believed there was nothing more for him to lose and, further, that he knew he would ultimately be destroyed by his monster. We are told that the judge was at first incredulous, concluding that the creature would be invulnerable to any use of force. However, he became intimidated by Victor's outraged appearance, and then gave assurances that he would help. Victor, however, was not convinced, and decided to take matters into his own hands, uttering words that echoed the monster's threats. "You refuse my just demand: I have but one resource; and I devote myself, either in my life or death, to his destruction." The chapter ends with Victor accusing the judge of suffering from "pride of wisdom," ironically, the same pride of which he is guilty.

Chapter VII begins with Victor leaving Geneva in order to pursue his monster. He reports that his state of mind was one of extreme agitation and that he was propelled into action out of pure revenge. "And now my wanderings had began, which are to cease but with life.... But revenge kept me alive." Victor first found himself at the cemetery where his loved ones were buried. Overcome with inconsolable grief, he knelt down to kiss the hallowed ground, vowing to avenge their unnatural and untimely deaths, and summoning the help of the spirits that appeared to be flitting around. At that very moment, his prayers were answered by a fiendish laugh. The monster appeared and whispered in Victor's ear that he is gratified his creator has decided to remain alive. Though Victor attempted to grasp him, the monster left with a supernatural swiftness.

Thus Victor's final pursuit began, taking him through the winding paths of the Rhône and the blue Mediterranean, where he boarded a vessel bound for the Black Sea and continued his chase through the wilds of Tartary and Russia. Though at times being fed by the local peasants, Victor endured the same cold, fatigue, and tortured mind that his creature previously experienced. Victor reports that his resolve was so fierce that he willingly accepted all manner of hardships. Sleep was his only sustenance as he dreamt of his loved ones. "Deprived of this respite, I should have sunk under my hardships. During the day I was sustained by and inspirited by the hope of night: for in sleep I saw my friends, my wife, and my beloved country."

For his part, the monster played sadistic games with Victor, taunting him with inscriptions left on the bark of trees in order to spur his creator into continuing his relentless pursuit. " 'My reign is not yet over,' (these words were legible in one of these inscriptions); 'you live, and my power is complete. Follow me; I seek the everlasting ices of the north, where you will feel the misery of cold and frost, to which I am impassive.' "

Without hesitation, Victor continued his pursuit northward toward an icy wilderness. His resolve was unshakable and his preparedness complete, having already procured a sleigh and dogs to cross the snow. Indeed, the wondrous speed at which he was able to traverse the ice allowed him to gain valuable ground he had previously lost. Eventually, Victor arrived at a "wretched hamlet" on the seashore and attempted to gather information from the local inhabitants as to the monster's whereabouts. They reported that the monster, threatening the residents with a gun and many pistols, caused the residents to flee while he stole their winter food supply and drove off on his sled with the aid of a pack of trained dogs. The villagers believed the monster to be dead by now since he drove off into a frozen wasteland. Victor's initial response to this news was a temporary despair that was soon dispelled by the perception that the creature has left victorious. "Yet at the idea that the fiend should live and be triumphant, my rage and vengeance returned, and, like a mighty tide, overwhelmed every other feeling." Victor then got himself a new sleigh and stocked up with provisions for his journey, a trip that he later calculated to be of three weeks duration based on the amount of food he consumed. Indeed, this latest venture into a land of immense and rugged mountains of ice had been so arduous that one of the animals that transported him died of fatigue. Shortly thereafter, Victor spotted the monster before him at barely a mile's distance. Unfortunately, Victor lost track of the monster once again, with the sea itself separating him from his enemy. During the following hours, several of Victor's dogs died, while he became increasingly dejected. It is at this juncture that he discovered Robert Walton's vessel at anchor and pleaded with him to kill the monster, since he expected that he would soon die. Warning Walton not to be seduced by the monster's fine rhetorical skills, he counsels him to remain steadfast in his resolve to destroy the creature. " 'He is eloquent and persuasive; and once his words had even power over my heart; but trust him not. His soul is as hellish as his form, full of treachery and fiend-like malice.' " **Chapter VII** now returns to the epistolary form as Robert Walton continues describing these fantastic events to his sister, Margaret. In a series of five short letters, Walton records the final events of Victor Frankenstein's story. The first letter, dated August 26th, 17__, continues to record Victor's anguished narration. For his part, Walton attaches credence to Victor's story, fully believing that the monster exists, as he observes Victor vacillating between moments of self-composure followed by sudden shrieking outbursts and, further, that Victor's narration is done in a coherent and sequential order. However, though he has inquired as to the secret of his creation, Victor categorically refused to divulge it, with the caveat that revealing the secret would only bring Walton to harm.

Ironically, while Walton was recording Victor's story, the otherwise distraught Victor Frankenstein became his editor, correcting and adding notes when necessary, another indication that Victor's psyche had been at least partially restored as a result of his confession. Robert finds much to admire in his guest and reports that the two had conversations about a wide range of literary matters in which Victor acquitted himself eloquently and movingly. "What a glorious creature must he have been in the days of his prosperity, when he is thus noble and godlike in ruin." At other moments, Victor's conversation reverted to a lamentation concerning the extreme hubris and excessive ambition that led to his current wretchedness, admonishing Walton to take heed.

In his second letter, dated September 2nd, Walton describes his enthusiasm for his own voyage, despite the treacherous conditions and a crew that has grown disheartened and frightened. "We may survive, and if we do not, I will repeat the lessons of my Seneca, and die with a good heart." However, Walton's passion and Victor's words of encouragement notwithstanding, his sailors demanded an immediate return home.

In his third letter, dated September 5th, Robert records Victor's declining health and the fear of mutiny from his crew unless he capitulated to their demands to turn homeward. Though encased in ice at that time, they told Walton that if these conditions were to change, they wanted him to turn south. For his part, Victor remonstrated with the men, exhorting them to continue the voyage as a mission marked by "lofty design and heroism."

In his fourth letter, dated September 7th, Walton concedes that he was obliged to return to England. "Thus are my hopes blasted by cowardice and indecision; I come back ignorant and disappointed.'"

In his fifth letter, dated September 12th, Walton reports that Victor had finally died following a steady decline in health, and that he has lost a cherished friend. In his final moments, Victor was sorely disappointed to learn that Walton planned to end the voyage, imploring him to pursue the monster and destroy it. Victor then bid his friend farewell, stating that he understood Walton's predicament, leaving him with some parting words of advice "'Seek happiness in tranquility, and avoid ambition, even if it be only the apparently innocent one of distinguishing yourself in science and discoveries.'"

Shortly after Victor's passing, Robert heard a voice in Victor's cabin, and discovered the monster, in all his enormous hideousness, standing over his creator's dead body, grieving his death. Though the monster headed for the window upon seeing Walton, the latter called him back, at which time the monster confessed the pity he felt for Victor, though the desire for revenge always took precedence. " 'Think ye that the groans of Clerval were music to my ears? My heart was fashioned to be susceptible of love and sympathy." For a moment, Walton was seduced by the monster's expressions of remorse, but remembering his friend's lifeless form, he lashed, branding the monster a "hypocritical fiend." Nevertheless, the monster still protested his innate goodness, blaming Victor's rejection and man's unkindness as the source of his evil. " 'Yet even the enemy of God and man had friends and associates in his desolation; I am quite alone.' " With no more purpose to live, the monster decided that he would kill himself by fire. "I ... shall seek the most northern extremity of the globe; I shall collect my funeral pile, and consume to ashes this miserable frame, that its remains may afford no light to any curious and unhallowed wretch, who would create such another as I have been." The monster, at last repentant, bid a grandiloquent farewell, stating that for all of Victor's suffering, his misery remained superior, and declaring that his death would yet be his triumph.

Notes

1. Alchemy, the origin of modern chemistry, was introduced to medieval Europe through translations of Arabic writings, where it became associated with heresy and witchcraft. In his pursuit of the philosopher's stone that would transform base metals into gold, and the elixir of life that would cheat death, the alchemist has always been a subversive figure in fact and in literature, a magician who sought to overturn the established authority and was perceived to be in league with the devil himself. Because of the fear they engendered and the consequent threats against their lives, the practitioners of alchemical arts were forced to pursue their work in secret, disguising their knowledge in obscure languages and symbols. Interest in alchemy would fade during the Enlightenment, and be revived by the Romantic imagination, which sought the union of self and Nature and argued for a vital wholeness in their poetry. Along with this Romantic concept of the union of self and Nature was the idea that what is internal in the individual is externally revealed in Nature and, thus, the alchemist's early attempts to perfect Nature were seen as

analogous to the Romantic notion of a redeemed selfhood, a process wholly internalized within the imagination. In his *Defence of Poetry* (1819), Percy Bysshe Shelley described the imagination as "mind acting upon ... thoughts so as to colour them with its own light, and composing them, as from elements, other thoughts."

2. The history of the University of Ingolstadt, so prominent in Victor Frankenstein's education, is an interesting one. Founded in 1472 by Duke Ludwig the Wealthy of Bavaria-Landshut, with a papal concession, the university was profoundly influenced by its Jesuit professors until they were suppressed in 1773. During the eighteenth century, however, the spirit of the Enlightenment brought an intellectual fervor to the university, most especially in the empirical sciences. This new spirit included the formation of a secret society known as the Illuminati whose goal was to study the means for bringing about a revolutionary reconstruction of European society. The Order of the Illuminati, whose name means "Enlightened Ones," was founded in 1776 by Adam Weishaupt, a former Jesuit and professor of canon law. The members of the society promoted a belief in deism and a doctrine of spiritual perfection. By the end of the eighteenth century, the Illuminati had essentially disbanded. Though they had little effect, the Illuminati remained a target for reactionary elements who blamed them for the French Revolution.

3. For purposes of this discussion, the sublime is here understood as those aspects of Nature and Art that affect the mind with a sense of overwhelming grandeur or irresistible power and that are calculated to inspire awe, deep reverence, or lofty emotion, by reason of beauty and grandeur. In the realm of ideas, it refers to the highest regions of thought, reality, or human activity.

CRITICAL VIEWS

PERCY BYSSHE SHELLEY ON *FRANKENSTEIN*[1]

The novel of 'Frankenstein; or, the Modern Prometheus,' is undoubtedly, as a mere story, one of the most original and complete productions of the day. We debate with ourselves in wonder, as we read it, what could have been the series of thoughts—what could have been the peculiar experiences that awakened them—which conduced, in the author's mind, to the astonishing combinations of motives and incidents, and the startling catastrophe, which compose this tale. There are, perhaps, some points of subordinate importance, which prove that it is the author's first attempt. But in this judgment, which requires a very nice discrimination, we may be mistaken; for it is conducted throughout with a firm and steady hand. The interest gradually, accumulates and advances towards the conclusion with the accelerated rapidity of a rock rolled down a mountain. We are led breathless with suspense and sympathy, and the heaping up of incident on incident, and the working of passion out of passion. We cry "hold, hold! enough!"—but there is yet something to come; and, like the victim whose history it relates, we think we can bear no more, and yet more is to be borne. Pelion is heaped on Ossa, and Ossa on Olympus. We climb Alp after Alp, until the horizon is seen blank, vacant, and limitless; and the head turns giddy, and the ground seems to fail under our feet.

This novel rests its claim on being a source of powerful and profound emotion. The elementary feelings of the human mind are exposed to view; and those who are accustomed to reason deeply on their origin and tendency will, perhaps, be the only persons who can sympathize, to the full extent, in the interest of the actions which are their result. But, founded on nature as they are, there is perhaps no reader who can endure anything beside a new love story, who will not feel a responsive string touched in his inmost soul. The sentiments are so affectionate and so innocent—the characters of the subordinate agents in this strange drama are clothed in the light of such a mild and gentle mind—the pictures of domestic manners are of the most simple and attaching character: the father's is irresistible and deep. Nor are the crimes and malevolence of the single Being, though indeed withering and tremendous, the offspring of any unaccountable propensity to evil, but flow irresistibly from certain causes fully adequate to their production. They are the children, as it were, of Necessity and Human Nature. In this the direct moral of the book consists; and it is perhaps the most important, and of the most universal application, of any moral that can be enforced by example. Treat a person ill, and he will become wicked. Requite affection with scorn;—let one being be selected, for whatever cause, as the refuse of his kind—divide him, a social being, from society, and you impose upon him the irresistible obligations—malevolence and selfishness. It is thus that, too often in society, those who are best qualified to be its benefactors and its ornaments, are branded by some accident with scorn, and changed, by neglect and solitude of heart, into a scourge and a curse.

The Being in 'Frankenstein' is, no doubt, a tremendous creature. It was impossible that he should not have received among men that treatment which led to the consequences of his being a social nature. He was an abortion and an anomaly; and though his mind was such as its first impressions framed it, affectionate and full of moral sensibility, yet the circumstances of his existence are so monstrous and uncommon, that, when the consequences of them became developed in action, his original goodness was gradually turned into inextinguishable misanthropy and revenge. The scene between the Being and the blind De Lacey in the cottage, is one of the most profound and extraordinary instances of pathos that we ever recollect. It is impossible to read this dialogue,—and indeed many others of a somewhat similar character,—without feeling the heart suspend its pulsations with wonder, and the "tears stream down the cheeks." The encounter and argument between Frankenstein and the Being on the sea of ice, almost approaches, in effect, to the expostulations of Caleb Williams with Falkland. It reminds us, indeed, somewhat of the style and character of that admirable writer, to whom the author has dedicated his work, and whose productions he seems to have studied.

There is only one instance, however, in which we detect the least approach to imitation; and that is the conduct of the incident of Frankenstein's landing in Ireland. The general character of the tale, indeed, resembles nothing that ever preceded it. After the death of Elizabeth, the story, like a stream which grows at once more rapid and profound as it proceeds, assumes an irresistible solemnity, and the magnificent energy and swiftness of a tempest.

The churchyard scene, in which Frankenstein visits the tombs of his family, his quitting Geneva, and his journey through Tartary to the shores of the Frozen Ocean, resemble at once the terrible reanimation of a corpse and the supernatural career of a spirit. The scene in the cabin of Walton's ship—the more than mortal enthusiasm and grandeur of the Being's speech over the dead body of his victim—is an exhibition of intellectual and imaginative power, which we think the reader will acknowledge has seldom been surpassed.

Note

1. Written in 1817; published (posthumously) in *The Athenaeum Journal of Literature, Science and the Fine Arts*, Nov. 10, 1832.

CROSBIE SMITH ON VICTOR'S GENEVESE YEARS

Eighteenth-century Enlightenment philosophers promoted the broad assumption that Nature was ordered and rational. Natural history, concerned with the *classification* of plants, of animals, of human beings, of stars, revealed the systematic arrangements within Nature. These patterns of order sometimes formed the basis for the famous 'design argument' in British natural theology (design *in* Nature demonstrates the existence and wisdom of God), and sometimes the basis for a de-Christianized deism that recognized an omniscient Designer.[8]

Natural philosophy, the study of the *laws* by which Nature acted or moved, complemented natural history. Investigations of the principles of regularities or uniformities of Nature, rather than Nature's hidden and ultimate causes, became standard for academic natural philosophers of the Age of Reason, with 'reason' itself being redefined as Natural Law. The Laws of Nature themselves, such as Newton's Law of universal gravitation, stood as the exemplars of Reason. Any further attempts to probe the causes 'behind' the law were then assigned to an ancient metaphysics (such as that of natural magic) and thus to *forbidden* territory.[9] Combining natural history (the arrangements) with natural philosophy (the laws of operation) yielded Nature's *economy*. In fact, Nature consisted of many economies or systems—the solar system, for example, or the plant economy. All of these natural economies, characterized by orderly arrangements and governed by immutable laws, acted in harmony with one another.

By the late eighteenth century, these various economies of Nature shared a common characteristic. They were all 'equilibrium systems', exemplified by the simple case of the lever or balance. The important feature was that in such systems slight disturbances would be compensated and adjusted in such a way that the equilibrium (or average) position was restored. Thus the phrase 'balance of Nature' was not just an empty cliché, but one that was related to actual systems in Nature.[10] Examples are numerous: Lavoisier's chemical equations that balanced quantitatively; D'Alembert's and Lagrange's reduction of the whole of the science of dynamics to that of statics or equilibrium through a so-called 'principle of virtual velocities', which was also exemplified in the Law of the lever; and Laplace's and Lagrange's new model of the solar system, in which planetary perturbations (thought by Newton to require God's restoring power) were shown to be periodical and self-restoring, such that the solar system would never fall into disorder.[11]

It followed that each system was a perfect system, operating like a perfect machine and capable of self-restoration. Such natural systems could thus form a model for the reform of other systems that showed anything but perfection, especially human institutions and societies. Nature stood as the exemplar of perfection amid human imperfection, but doctrines of the 'perfectibility of man' meant that human beings could at least aspire to such perfection by reforming or even overthrowing unnatural tyranny and authoritarian systems in favour of free individuals in a new state of nature, with each individual pursuing life, liberty and happiness and thereby maximizing the sum total of human happiness.[12]

These doctrines presupposed that man, thus set free, would act as a rational creature, seeking to optimize his own interests but not at too great an expense to other rational creatures. In John Locke's words (*pace* Hobbes), 'the state of Nature has a law of Nature to govern it, which obliges everyone ... that being all equal and independent, no one ought to harm another in his life, health, liberty or possessions'.[13] A perfect human economy would also act like a balanced machine, and small variations would only lead to fluctuations around a natural mean.

The notion of a balanced economy of nature, however, carried with it something more than benevolent harmony: Nemesis, the goddess of retribution. Traditional views persisted in the work of, for instance, the celebrated eighteenth-century botanist-classifier Carl Linnaeus (1707–78). *Divine nemesis* would act to prevent a loss of equilibrium in Nature's economies. All levels of Nature and society needed to be maintained within their 'proper limits' so as to prevent evil—entailing chaos and disorder—triumphing over good, the latter understood in terms of order, balance and happiness.

The clergyman Thomas Robert Malthus (1766–1834) offered a similar perspective around 1800. The sexual appetites of living creatures led to a tendency towards ever-expanding populations according to a geometrical increase. But the arithmetical increase in food supply provided a natural check on any given population, such that a balance was always maintained with respect to a given species. The benefits to the whole economy of nature were obvious: no single species could overrun the world. But the price paid in terms of suffering, starvation and death by individuals (especially human individuals) by allowing free reign to their populating urges could be very high indeed. This kind of nemesis derived principally from God through the system established by Him for ordering Nature and society. But more radical 'secular' philosophers tended to view the laws of Nature as sufficient guides to morality. Violation of natural law and disobedience to her systems would bring Nature's retribution on the 'evil-doer'.[14]

From the opening of the very first chapter of Victor Frankenstein's personal account, readers learn that his family origins combined all the values of enlightened Swiss respectability and stability:

> I am by birth a Genevese; and my family is one of the most distinguished of that republic. My ancestors had been for many years counsellors and syndics [legislators]; and my father [Alphonse] had filled several public situations with honour and reputation. He was respected by all who knew him for his integrity and indefatigable attention to public business. He passed his younger days perpetually occupied by the affairs of his country; and it was not until the decline of life that he thought of marrying, and bestowing on the state sons who might carry his virtues and his name down to posterity.

And, as Victor added later, the 'republican institutions of our country have produced simpler and happier manners than those which prevail in the great monarchies that surround it'.[15] Victor's father, then, was a man of impeccable republican credentials, a man prepared to sacrifice self-promotion and self-gratification for the public good. Even marriage was to serve the interests of the state by allowing the perpetuation of virtue, embodied in the name of Frankenstein, to posterity. Indeed, the Frankensteins were construed as guardians of virtue rather than individuals employing, as Victor would employ, virtue as a means to power and self-aggrandisement.

Alphonse Frankenstein displayed those very qualities of nobility and honour in the events that led to his marriage to Caroline Beaufort, daughter of an old merchant friend.

Beaufort's slide from prosperity into poverty prompted the merchant, following honourable settlement of his debts, to retreat into a wretched state of isolation from society. Sacrificing all self-interest in the search for his friend, Alphonse arrived too late to save the old man from death, but 'came like a protecting spirit to the poor girl, who committed herself to his care'.[16] Following marriage to Caroline, Alphonse sacrificed his public employments to the call of domestic duty, devoting himself to the education of his children. Victor, the eldest child, expressed the state of family stability and happiness thus: 'No creature could have more tender parents than mine. My improvement and health were their constant care, especially as I remained for several years their only child'.[17]

Into this ideal domestic state came the abandoned Elizabeth, Victor's cousin and future fiancée. Indeed, it was Victor's mother who, desiring 'to bind as closely as possible the ties of domestic love', had decided 'to consider Elizabeth as my future wife'. The immediate result was a powerful reinforcement of domestic equilibrium and happiness:

> If the servants had any request to make, it was always through her intercession. We [Elizabeth and Victor] were strangers to any species of disunion and dispute; for although there was a great dissimilitude in our characters, there was a harmony in that very dissimilitude. I was more calm and philosophical than my companion; yet my temper was not so yielding. My application was of longer endurance; but it was not so severe whilst it endured. I delighted in investigating the facts relative to the actual world; she busied herself in following the aërial creations of the poets. The world was to me a secret, which I desired to discover; to her it was a vacancy, which she sought to people with imaginations of her own.[18]

Already, of course, Victor's listeners are given a hint that something dark lurked in Victor's nature, perhaps even within Nature itself, in contrast to the outward stability, harmony and delights of conventional and enlightened domestic society, where even the servants could share in the state of happiness. But in the meantime, 'No youth could have passed more happily than mine. My parents were indulgent, and my companions amiable'.[19]

Notes

8. Crosbie Smith, 'From Design to Dissolution: Thomas Chalmers' Debt to John Robison', *British Journal for the History of Science*, XII (1979), pp. 59–70 (on natural history, natural philosophy and natural theology); J. H. Brooke, *Science and Religion: Some Historical Perspectives* (Cambridge, 1991), pp. 191–225 (on the fortunes and functions of natural theology in the early nineteenth century).

9. T. L. Hankins, *Science and the Enlightenment* (Cambridge, 1985), pp. 3–7 (on Reason and natural law); Richard Kieckhefer, *Magic in the Middle Ages* (Cambridge, 1989), p. 9 (on natural magic as a science of hidden powers).

10. M. N. Wise (with the collaboration of Crosbie Smith), 'Work and Waste: Political Economy and Natural Philosophy in Nineteenth-Century Britain (1)', *History of Science*, XXVII (1989), pp. 263–301 (pp. 266–8).

11. Ibid., pp. 268–75.

12.. Ibid., pp. 272–5, 288.

13. John Locke, *Of Civil Government* (1690), cited in Gerd Buchdahl, *The Image of Newton and Locke in the Age of Reason* (London, 1961), pp. 91–2.

14. Wise (with Smith), *op. cit.*, pp. 278, 281–2.

15. Shelley, *The 1818 Text*, pp. 17, 46.

16. Ibid., pp. 17–19.

17. Ibid., p. 19.

18. Ibid., p. 29.

19. Ibid., p. 21.

LUDMILLA JORDANOVA ON MELANCHOLY REFLECTION

When Frankenstein finally left his secluded home for the University of Ingolstadt following his mother's death, his feelings were ambivalent—loss combined with desire:

I ... indulged in the most melancholy reflection.... I was now alone. My life had hitherto been remarkably secluded

71

and domestic.... I believed myself totally unfitted for the company of strangers.... as I proceeded, my spirits and hopes rose. I ardently desired the acquisition of knowledge.... my desires were complied with....[1]

Shelley's choice of the term 'melancholy' was apt, since it encapsulated ambivalence. Although it suggested sad, gloomy and mournful feelings, it also evoked a sense of pleasure, of the delicious self-indulgence of such feelings. Melancho*lia* was a disease, a neurosis, in the terminology of William Cullen, 'characterised by erroneous judgement'. One image of melancholy, a looser term, which in the early nineteenth century carried both medical and general emotional connotations, associated it with refined, learned and civilized men. While melancholy could be pathological, it also expressed the superior sensibilities of an intellectual elite.[2] Frankenstein's inability to keep his intimate, domestic self in a healthy balance with his thirst for knowledge, both of which had a melancholic aspect, constitutes the central monstrosity that the novel explores.

Far from being a simple moralistic tale of masculinist, scientific overreaching, drawing on simple definitions of 'science', 'medicine' or 'surgery', *Frankenstein* is a remarkably precise exploration of the internal conflicts felt by practitioners in a variety of fields, which we can conveniently yoke together as 'natural knowledge', and which are examined by Shelley with acuity. These conflicts are also historically specific, since they surfaced at a time when the expectations and claims of men of science and of medicine were disproportionate to their actual status and power. This mismatch was all the more frustrating because the idiom of scientific heroism, which became increasingly widely available in the first three decades of the nineteenth century, was enticing and seductive, yet insufficiently backed up by state support and cultural rewards.[3] Instability, uncertainty, ambiguity—these are key themes of Shelley's text, and they are explored with particular power through the account of his life that Frankenstein gives to Walton. Walton's character, like Frankenstein's, is portrayed as an uneasy mix. On the one hand he is a daring explorer, a student of nature, possessed of an 'ardent curiosity' and of a desire to triumph over the elements, while on the other he is an isolated, lonely daydreamer, who is ultimately a failure. Walton and Frankenstein recognize their kinship, as the latter asks the former: 'Do you share my madness?'[4]

In order to pursue this argument I need to advance on two fronts, first by discussing the key chapters of Shelley's text, and second by analysing some of the issues portrayals of 'scientists' and 'doctors' raised in her time. Here we must note the anachronism if not of 'doctor' then certainly of 'scientist'. Although the term itself was not coined until the 1830s, there was none the less a sense well before then of men grouped together into some kind of collective, with shared concerns and values, and above all with a common epistemology.[5] This feeling of commonality, well before the word 'scientist' was current among those who produced natural knowledge, is a significant phenomenon. We might cite in support of this point the oil painting *Men of Science Now Living* (1807–8), in London's National Portrait Gallery, which was an attempt to represent a collective and national achievement by means of a group portrait assembled from existing images of those selected as worthy of inclusion.[6]

In Mary Shelley's treatment, what is common to the different pursuits Frankenstein is enthused by is their capacity to open up nature's secrets, or at least they are designed to do so. They reveal or unveil something, personified as female, and presented as mysterious, enticing and potent. I wish to concentrate on the first four chapters, in which Frankenstein narrates his life until the time he is on the brink of completing his creation. From these chapters six themes, all of overriding importance for my argument, emerge. First, seclusion and reclusiveness; these characterize his early family life long before he undertakes his solitary work on making the 'monster'. Second, passion. Even as a child he is described as having a temper, being passionate, and throughout the account of his life his strong desires are foregrounded, above all his desire to learn the secrets of heaven and earth, to possess a kind of knowledge that is full of grandeur. These aspects of his personality were presented by Mary Shelley as overwhelming him, as forces he could not resist or control. Third, there was an absence of satisfaction. Frankenstein was often left unsatisfied by the activities he undertook, by the knowledge available to him, and accordingly he is set apart from others, suffering an inner emptiness. Fourth, he was drawn to particular kinds of natural knowledge. It is striking that he felt attracted to domains that were marginal, contentious or on the boundaries of what could be controlled, such as alchemy and electricity, and that he changed his mind so often about what interested him. This intellectual fickleness led him to discard areas in emotive terms: 'I at once gave up my former occupations, set down natural history and all its progeny as a deformed and abortive creation'.[7] Here fields of knowledge are treated in the way his monster was to be. Fifth, Frankenstein had powerful responses—both positive and negative—to those in positions of intellectual authority over him: his father, his father's friend who explained electricity to him, and his two, very different, teachers at Ingolstadt: Krempe, who repels him, and Waldman, to whom he feels drawn. It is important to note that in the last case this included a strong *physical* reaction to their persons and demeanour. Shelley's account gives credence to the idea that the character of men of science was to be 'read' in their appearance. It was also to be 'read' in their signatures, which were often reproduced beneath their printed portraits.[8]

Finally, the history of natural knowledge is given prominence. The contentious nature of some of the areas to which Frankenstein is attracted derives from the fact that they are archaic: they belong to a past, not a present. Specific mention is made of Cornelius Agrippa, Paracelsus and Albertus Magnus. Humphry Davy's *Elements of Chemical Philosophy*, which Mary Shelley read in 1816, opened with a 'Historical View of the Progress of Chemistry'. His purpose there was to place earlier chemical traditions, including alchemy, in a broad framework, which defined how proper chemical knowledge was to be acquired, specified its usefulness to humankind, and asserted its status as part of an 'intelligent design of the system of the earth'. For Davy, history helps to reveal the stable aspect of experiment, which 'is as it were the chain that binds down the Proteus of nature, and obliges it to confess its real form and divine origin'.[9] For Frankenstein, history and experiment had released an aberrant form of nature, whose origins are profane. Furthermore, Frankenstein revealed his scepticism about the 'modern professors of natural science'.[10] It is true that this refers to his early years, but Frankenstein's evocation of a sense of there being a *history* to natural knowledge is nonetheless significant: 'I had retrod the steps of knowledge along the paths of time ...'.[11] His sense of history was reinforced by Waldman, who 'began his lecture by a recapitulation of the history of chemistry', as did many lecturers in the eighteenth century. And what really inspired Frankenstein was Waldman's way of presenting 'the ancient teachers of science' as mere speculators, and 'the modern masters' as the real miracle-workers.[12] The appeal of performing miracles and probing secrets is still there, but now, thanks to Waldman, it is associated with the moderns. Yet, Waldman's humanity allows the historical figures others dismissed to become those who laid 'the foundations' of modern knowledge. A historical perspective allowed Frankenstein to embrace the present, which he had previously rejected. Here, as elsewhere in the book, Shelley explored different modes of knowledge, not in order to rank and evaluate them, but rather to probe their moral and psychic qualities.

One possible reading of Shelley's depiction of Frankenstein's development and inner life is as an unambiguously critical portrayal of perverted science. And it could be added that it bears no resemblance to the behaviour of medical practitioners and students of nature at the time she was writing. I want to suggest that, on the contrary, she was acutely sensitive to areas of uncertainty and ambiguity felt by those who studied medicine and/or the natural sciences and whose relations with the past of their 'disciplines' were being carefully negotiated at just this time. Many practitioners wrote histories precisely in order to work out the extent of their debt to the ancients and to their other forebears, to give a perspective to 'modern' achievements, to place themselves in a lineage.[13] This was important precisely because they felt deeply implicated by the past, which was not yet separate enough to be put aside safely, but was still sufficiently 'close' to require active management. Those who studied medicine at universities had to read some of the ancients very closely indeed; they would have been well aware of attempts to give a shape to the history of their field, which included compilations and codifications of medical writings.[14] It was because savants felt vulnerable to the suggestion that magic, and an improper concern with death and the supernatural, were still part of the scientific enterprise that they felt the need to repudiate them so firmly. Debates about physiognomy, with its troubling kinship with divination, mesmerism and the violent contests over definitions of 'quackery' can all be characterized in these terms.[15]

Notes

1. Mary Shelley, *Frankenstein* (Harmondsworth, 1985), p. 89. All subsequent references to Shelley's text are from this edition, edited by Maurice Hindle, hereafter cited as *Frankenstein*.

2. Robert Morris, James Kendrick and others, *Edinburgh Medical and Physical Dictionary* (Edinburgh, 1807); the definition of 'melancholia' is in volume II, not paginated. Definitions of melancholy and its cognates in the *OED* are also illuminating. On melancholy see W. Lepenies, *Melancholy and Society* (Cambridge, MA, 1992). Some paintings by Joseph Wright of Derby could be said to touch on 'melancholy' in their exploration of the relationships between natural knowledge, the boundaries between life and death, contemplation and introspection. Indeed, Wright's *Hermit Studying Anatomy* of 1771–3 was used for the cover of the Penguin edition of *Frankenstein*. Equally interesting are *The Alchemist, in Search of the Philosopher's Stone, Discovers Phosphorus* (exh. 1771; reworked and dated '1791'), *Miravan Opening the Tomb of his Ancestors* (1772), the portrait *Brooke Boothby* (1781), and *The Indian Widow* (1785); see B. Nicolson, *Joseph Wright of Derby: Painter of Light*, 2 vols (London, 1968), and *Wright of Derby*, exh. cat. ed. J. Egerton; London, Tate Gallery; Paris, Grand Palais; New York, Metropolitan Museum of Art; 1990. It is perhaps significant that Wright painted Erasmus Darwin, who is so often mentioned in connection with *Frankenstein*, five times.

3. L. S. Jacyna, 'Images of John Hunter in the Nineteenth Century', *History of Science*, XXI (1983), pp. 85–108; S. Schaffer, 'Genius in Romantic Natural Philosophy', in *Romanticism and the Sciences*, ed. A. Cunningham and N. Jardine (Cambridge, 1990), pp.

82–98; D. Knight, 'The Scientist as Sage', *Studies in Romanticism*, VI (1967), pp. 65–88. See also A. Desmond, *The Politics of Evolution: Morphology, Medicine and Reform in Radical London* (Chicago, 1989).

4. *Frankenstein*, p. 73.

5. It is sometimes said that Coleridge coined the term 'scientist' in 1833; for example in T. Levere, 'Coleridge and the Sciences', in *Romanticism and the Sciences* (Cambridge, 1990) pp. 295–306, especially p. 296, but see also R. Williams, *Keywords: A Vocabulary of Culture and Society* (revd edn London, 1983), pp. 276–80, especially p. 279, where Williams attributes it to Whewell in 1840. Williams notes that the word 'scientist' was used very occasionally in the late eighteenth century.

6. Richard Walker, *Regency Portraits* (London, 1985), I, pp. 605–8; II, plates 516–24, NPG nos. 1075, 1075a, 1075b and 1383a.

7. *Frankenstein*, p. 86.

8. The most important source for scientific and medical portraits is Renate Burgess, *Portraits of Doctors and Scientists in the Wellcome Institute of the History of Medicine* (London, 1973); my impression is that signatures were particularly likely to be added to portraits when prints were published as frontispieces to be collected works of medical authors or as illustrations to obituaries. Recent work on French eulogies is also relevant: Dorinda Outram, 'The Language of Natural Power: The "Eloges" of Georges Cuvier and the Public Language of Nineteenth Century Science', *History of Science*, XVI (1978), pp. 153–78; Daniel Roche, 'Talent, Reason, and Sacrifice: The Physician during the Enlightenment', in *Medicine and Society in France*, ed. R. Forster and O. Ranum (Baltimore, 1980), pp. 66–88; C. Paul, *Science and Immortality: The Eloges of the Paris Academy of Sciences (1699–1791)* (Berkeley, 1980).

9. Humphry Davy, *Elements of Chemical Philosophy* (London, 1812), p. 503; the 'Historical View of the Progress of Chemistry' is pp. 1–60. On Mary Shelley's reading see N. White, *Shelley* (London, 1947), II, pp. 539–45, and P. Feldman and D. Scott-Kilvert, eds, *The Journals of Mary Shelley 1814–1844* (Oxford, 1987), I, pp. 85–103. Hindle comments on her reading of Davy: *Frankenstein*, pp. 24–5.

10. *Frankenstein*, p. 91.

11. Ibid.

12. Ibid., p. 92.

13. C. Webster, 'The Historiography of Medicine' in *Information Sources in the History of Science and Medicine* (London, 1983), pp. 29–43; J. Christie, 'The Development of the Historiography of Science', in *Companion to the History of Modern Science*, ed. R. Olby, G. Cantor, J. Christie and M. Hodge (London, 1990), pp. 5–22.

14. L. Rosner, *Medical Education in the Age of Improvement: Edinburgh Students and Apprentices, 1760–1850* (Edinburgh, 1991),

conveys most effectively the ways in which medical students encountered the ancients and the more modern masters.

15. L. Jordanova, 'The Art and Science of Seeing in Medicine: Physiognomy 1780–1820', in *Medicine and the Five Senses*, ed. W. Bynum and R. Porter (Cambridge, 1993) pp. 122–33; R. Darnton, *Mesmerism and the End of the Enlightenment in France* (Cambridge, MA, 1968); R. Porter, *Health for Sale: Quackery in England, 1660–1850* (Manchester, 1989).

ANNE K. MELLOR ON THE MODERN PROMETHEUS

When Mary Shelley subtitled her novel "The Modern Prometheus," she forcefully directed our attention to the book's critique both of the promethean poets she knew best, Byron and Percy Shelley, and of the entire Romantic ideology as she understood it. Victor Frankenstein's failure to mother his child has both political and aesthetic ramifications. The father who neglects his children can be seen as the archetype of the irresponsible political leader who puts his own interests ahead of those of his fellow citizens. Victor Frankenstein's quest is nothing less than the conquest of death itself. By acquiring the ability to "bestow animation upon lifeless matter" and thus "renew life where death had apparently devoted the body to corruption" (49), Frankenstein in effect hopes to become God, the creator of life and the gratefully worshipped father of a new race of immortal beings. In his attempt to transform human beings into deities by eliminating mortality, Victor Frankenstein is himself participating in the mythopoeic vision that inspired the first generation of Romantic poets and thinkers. William Blake had insisted that the human form could become divine through the exercise of mercy, pity, love, and imagination; Coleridge had stated that human perception or the primary imagination is an "echo of the Infinite I AM;" Wordsworth had argued that the "higher minds" of poets are "truly from the Deity;" while both Godwin and his disciple Percy Shelley had proclaimed that man was perfectible. In their view, the right use of reason and imagination could annihilate not only social injustice and human evil but even, through participation

78

in symbolic thinking or what Blake called the "divine analogy," the consciousness of human finitude and death itself.[1] Victor Frankenstein's goal can be identified with the radical desire that energized some of the best known English Romantic poems, the desire to elevate human beings into living gods.

In identifying Victor Frankenstein with Prometheus, Mary Shelley was alluding to both versions of the Prometheus myth: Prometheus *plasticator* and Prometheus *pyrphoros*. In the first version, known to Mary Shelley through Ovid's *Metamorphoses* which she read in 1815, Prometheus created man from clay:

> Whether with particles of Heav'nly fire
> The God of Nature did his Soul inspire,
> Or Earth, but new divided from the Skie,
> And, pliant, still, retain'd the Aethereal Energy;
> Which Wise *Prometheus* temper'd into paste,
> And mix't with living Streams, the Godlike Image caste ...
> From such rude Principles our Form began;
> And Earth was Metamorphos'd into Man. (I:101–6, 111–12)

In the alternate, more famous version of the myth, Prometheus is the fire-stealer, the god who defied Jupiter's tyrannical oppression of humanity by giving fire to man and was then punished by having his liver eaten by vultures until he divulged his secret foreknowledge of Jupiter's downfall. By the third century A.D., these two versions had fused; the fire stolen by Prometheus became the fire of life with which he animated his man of clay.[2] As both the creator and/or savior of man and the long-suffering rebel against tyranny, Prometheus was an often invoked self-image among the Romantic poets. Blake visually identified his heroic rebel and spokeswoman Oothoon with the tortured Prometheus in his design for Plate 6 of "Visions of the Daughters of Albion," while Coleridge's Ancient Mariner echoes Prometheus both in his transgression of an established moral order and in his perpetual suffering that he may teach mankind to be both sadder and wiser. Even more directly, Goethe in both his verse drama *Prometheus* and his monologue "Bedecke deinen Himmel, Zeus" portrayed

Prometheus as a self-portrait of the artist who has liberated himself from serving dull, idle gods and who rejoices instead in his own creative powers.

Mary Shelley specifically associated her modern Prometheus with the Romantic poets she knew personally. During the summer in which she began writing *Frankenstein*, Byron composed his poem "Prometheus," a celebration of the god's defiance of Jupiter which emphasizes Prometheus' unyielding will, noble suffering, and concern for mankind—qualities with which Byron clearly identified himself.[3] Mary Shelley copied this poem and carried it to Byron's publisher John Murray when she returned to England in August 1816. Byron's Promethean persona appeared again in *Manfred*, which Mary Shelley read soon after its publication on June 16, 1817. Manfred's Faustian thirst for unbounded experience, knowledge, and freedom leads him, like Victor Frankenstein, to steal the secrets of nature. As Manfred confesses:

[I] dived,
In my lone wanderings, to the caves of death,
Searching its cause in its effect; and drew
From wither'd bones, and skulls, and heap'd up dust,
Conclusions most forbidden.
  (*Manfred* II. ii. 173–77)

Manfred's quest also enchained him in a Promethean suffering for his lost sister Astarte, a painful remorse that articulates Byron's guilty conscience over his incestuous affair with his half-sister Augusta Leigh. In his defiance of Ahrimanes and all other deities, Manfred proclaims Byron's personal belief in the ultimate creative power and integrity of the human imagination, using phrases that Mary Shelley condensed into that single "spark of being" infused by her modern Prometheus into the lifeless creature at his feet:

The mind, the spirit, the Promethean spark,
The lightning of my being, is as bright,
Pervading, and far darting as your own,

And shall not yield to yours, though coop'd in clay!
(*Manfred* I. i. 154–57)

In England, Mary Shelley met another poet who became a close friend and associate of both Byron and the Shelleys, Leigh Hunt, who intensified the identification of the Romantic poet with the Prometheus myth. Hunt commented in 1819 after the publication of *Frankenstein* that he too had thought of writing a poem entitled *Prometheus Throned* in which Prometheus would successfully defy the gods and be depicted as "having lately taken possession of Jupiter's seat."[4]

Above all, Mary Shelley associated her modern Prometheus with Percy Shelley, who had already announced his desire to compose an epic rebuttal to Aeschylus' *Prometheus Bound* when he reread the play in 1816, although he did not begin writing *Prometheus Unbound* until September 1818, after *Frankenstein* was published.[5] As William Veeder has most recently reminded us, several dimensions of Victor Frankenstein are modelled directly from Percy Shelley.[6] Victor was Percy Shelley's penname for his first publication, *Original Poetry; by Victor and Cazire* (1810). Victor Frankenstein's family resembles Percy Shelley's: in both, the father is married to a woman young enough to be his daughter; in both the oldest son has a favorite sister (adopted sister, or cousin, in Frankenstein's case) named Elizabeth. Frankenstein's education is based on Percy Shelley's: both were avid students of Albertus Magnus, Paracelsus, Pliny, and Buffon; both were fascinated by alchemy and chemistry; both were excellent linguists, acquiring fluency in Latin, Greek, German, French, English, and Italian.[7] By sending Victor Frankenstein to the University of Ingolstadt, Mary Shelley further signalled his association with the radical politics advocated by Percy Shelley in *Queen Mab* (1813), "Feelings of a Republican on the Fall of Bonapart" (1816), and *Laon and Cythna* (1817). Ingolstadt was famous as the home of the Illuminati, a secret revolutionary society founded in 1776 by Ingolstadt's Professor of Law, Adam Weishaupt, that advocated the perfection of mankind through the overthrow of established religious and political institutions. Percy Shelley had eagerly endorsed Weishaupt's goals—namely, "to secure to merit its just rewards; to the weak support, to the wicked the fetters they deserve; and to man his dignity" by freeing all men from the slavery imposed by "society, governments, the sciences, and false religion"—when he read Abbé Barruel's vitriolic attack on the Illuminati, *Mémoires, pour servir à L'Histoire du Jacobinisme* (1797), during his honeymoon journey with Mary in 1814. He had even used Barruel's account of the Illuminati, reading white where Barruel wrote black, as the basis of the utopian society depicted in the novel entitled *The Assassins* that he began during the summer of 1814.[8]

More important, Victor Frankenstein embodies certain elements of Percy Shelley's temperament and character that had begun to trouble Mary Shelley. She perceived in Percy an intellectual hubris or belief in the supreme importance of mental abstractions that led him to be insensitive to the feelings of those who did not share his ideas and enthusiasms. The Percy Shelley that Mary knew and loved lived in a world of abstract ideas; his actions were primarily motivated by theoretical principles, the quest for perfect beauty, love, freedom, goodness. While Mary endorsed and shared these goals, she had come to suspect that in Percy's case they sometimes masked an emotional narcissism, an unwillingness to confront the origins of his own desires or the impact of his demands on those most dependent upon him. Percy's pressure on Mary, during the winter and spring of 1814–15, to take Hogg as a lover despite her sexual indifference to Hogg; his indifference to the death of Mary's first baby on March 7, 1815; his insistence on Claire's continuing presence in his household despite Mary's stated opposition—all this had alerted Mary to a worrisome strain of selfishness in Percy's character, an egotism that too often rendered him an insensitive husband and an uncaring, irresponsible parent.

Percy Shelley's self-serving "harem psychology" may have originated as some Freudian critics have suggested, in an unresolved Oedipal desire to possess the mother. This desire emerges in his poem "Alastor" (1816) as a wish to return to the gravelike womb of Mother Earth. Mary Shelley's insight into this dimension of Percy's psyche informs the dream she assigns to Victor Frankenstein immediately after the creation of the monster:

> I thought I saw Elizabeth, in the bloom of health, walking in the streets of Ingolstadt. Delighted and surprised, I embraced her; but as I imprinted the first kiss on her lips, they became livid with the hue of death; her features appeared to change, and I thought that I held the corpse of my dead mother in my arms; a shroud enveloped her form, and I saw the grave-worms crawling in the folds of the flannel. (53)

Notes

1. See Anne K. Mellor, *Blake's Human Form Divine* (Berkeley: University of California Press, 1974), for a discussion of the "divine analogy" and the "human form divine" in William Blake's poetry and art.

2. Ovid's *Metamorphoses*, Book I, lines 101–6, 111–12, translated by John Dryden, *The Works of John Dryden*, ed. A. B. Chambers and W. Frost (Berkeley: University of California Press, 1974), IV:378–79. For Mary Shelley's reading of Ovid, see her *Journal*, ed. Frederick L. Jones (Norman, Oklahoma: University of Oklahoma Press, 1947), entries between April 8–May 13, 1815, pp. 43–47. Burton Pollin first identified Ovid as Mary Shelley's source for the Prometheus plasticator myth, "Philosophical and Literary Sources of *Frankenstein*," *Comparative Literature* 17 (1965): 102. For helpful discussions of the use of the Prometheus myth in *Frankenstein*, see David Ketterer, *Frankenstein's Creation: The Book, the Monster, and the Human Reality* (Victoria, British Columbia: Victoria University Press—English Literature Studies Number 16, 1979); and M. K. Joseph, Introduction to the 1831 edition of *Frankenstein, or The Modern Prometheus* (Oxford and New York: Oxford University Press, 1969, repr. 1984).

3. Byron had long admired Aeschylus' *Prometheus Bound*, which he asked Percy Shelley to translate from the Greek for him in July, 1816. In "Prometheus," Byron both identifies Prometheus as "a symbol and a sign / To Mortals of their fate and force" (ll. 45–46) and projects his own distress at his divorce and the loss of his daughter into his description of Prometheus' "silent suffering": "All that the proud can feel of pain, / The agony they do not show, / The suffocating sense of woe, / Which speaks but in its loneliness" (lines 8–11; Diodati, July 1816).

The link between Victor Frankenstein and Byron is further strengthened in the 1831 edition, where Mary Shelley borrows Byron's self-image of the poet as a greater Newton, no longer picking up pebbles on the seashore but venturing out onto the "ocean of eternity" (*Don Juan* 10:4), for Frankenstein himself:

> "I have described myself as always having been embued with a fervent longing to penetrate the secrets of nature. In spite of the intense labour and wonderful discoveries of modern philosophers, I always came from my studies discontented and unsatisfied. Sir Isaac Newton is said to have avowed that he felt like a child picking up shells beside the great and unexplored ocean of truth. Those of his successors in each branch of natural philosophy with whom I was acquainted, appeared even to my boy's apprehensions, as tyros engaged in the same pursuit" (238).

4. *Shelley and His Circle 1773–1822*, ed. Kenneth Neill Cameron and Donald H. Reiman (Cambridge: Harvard University Press, 1961–73), VI:841.

5. *Mary Shelley's Journal*, ed. Frederick L. Jones, p.73 Mary Shelley's perception of a link between Aeschylus' *Prometheus Bound*, Percy Shelley's poetic persona, and her own novel may underlie her journal entry for July 13, 1817: "Shelley translates 'Prometheus Desmotes' and I write it" (Bodleian Library: Abinger MS. Dep. d. 311/2). This entry is erroneously printed in *Mary Shelley's Journal*, p. 82.

6. Peter Dale Scott, "Vital Artifice: Mary, Percy, and the Psychopolitical Integrity of *Frankenstein*," *The Endurance of Frankenstein*, ed. George Levine and U. C. Knoepflmacher (Berkeley and Los Angeles, and London: University of California Press, 1979), pp. 175–83; William Veeder, *Mary Shelley & Frankenstein—The Fate of Androgyny* (Chicago: University of Chicago Press, 1986), pp. 92–95, 112–23, passim. See also Christopher Small, *Ariel Like a Harpy: Shelley, Mary and Frankenstein* (London: Gollancz, 1972); Richard Holmes, *Shelley—The Pursuit* (New York: E. P. Dutton, 1975), pp. 331–32; and Judith Weissman, "A Reading of *Frankenstein* as the Complaint of a Political Wife," *Colby Library Quarterly* XII (December 1976): 171–80.

7. For Percy Shelley's reading of Albertus Magnus, Paracelsus, Pliny, and Buffon, see Newman Ivey White, *Shelley* (London: Secker and Warburg, 1941; revised edition, 1947), I:41, 50–52, 158; on Shelley's obsession with alchemy and chemistry, see Thomas Jefferson Hogg's account of his Oxford days, *The Life of Percy Bysshe Shelley* (London: Edward Moxon, 1858), I:33–34, 58–76.

8. On the association of the Illuminati and the University of Ingolstadt, see Ludwig Hammermayer, "Die letzte Epoche der Universität Ingolstadt: Reformer, Jesuiten, Illuminaten (1746–1800)," in *Ingolstadt: Die Herzogsstadt—Die Universitätsstadt—Die Festung*, ed. Theodor Müller and Wilhelm Reissmüller (Ingolstadt: Verlag Donau Courier, 1974), pp. 299–357. The goals of the Illuminati are stated by L'Abbé Augustin Barruel in *Memoirs, Illustrating the History of Jacobinism*, trans. Robert Clifford (London, 1797–98), III:117, 228. For Percy Shelley's reading of Barruel, see *Mary Shelley's Journal*, ed. Federick L. Jones, entries for 23, 25 August and 9, 11 October, 1814. On Percy Shelley's use of Weishaupt's revolutionary doctrines, see Gerald McNiece, *Shelley and the Revolutionary Idea* (Cambridge: Harvard University Press, 1969), pp. 22–23, 97–101. For an account of Percy Shelley's revolutionary doctrines in "The Assassins," see Newman Ivey White, *Shelley*, I:682–83. On the impact of Barruel on *Frankenstein*, see Burton R. Pollin, "Sources of *Frankenstein*," p. 103 n23; and Horst Meller, "Prometheus im romantischen Heiligen-Kalender," in *Antike Tradition und Neuere Philologien*, ed. Hans-Joachim Simmermann (Heidelberg: Carl Winter-Universitätsverlag, 1984), pp. 163–69.

DAVID KETTERER ON THE SUBLIME SETTING

Of major relevance to an understanding of Mary's perception and description of landscape is an awareness of eighteenth-century theories of the picturesque and the sublime. The difference is largely one of scale. A picturesque landscape reinforces human values and operates within human dimensions. A sublime landscape suggests a much enlarged order of reality. Descending the Rhine with Clerval below Mainz, where it "becomes much more picturesque" (p. 155), Frankenstein records an unexpected alternation of the sublime and the homely picturesque: "In one spot you view rugged hills, ruined castles overlooking tremendous precipices, with the dark Rhine rushing beneath; and on the sudden turn of a promontory, flourishing vineyards with green sloping banks and a meandering river and populous towns occupy the scene." For Clerval, the essentially picturesque nature of the German landscape is reassuring: "Oh, surely, the spirit that inhabits and guards this place has a soul more in harmony with man, than those who pile the glacier or retire to the inaccessible peaks of the mountains of our own country" (p. 156).

But in *Frankenstein* the picturesque setting is infrequent and always something of a cheat. The sense of security it arouses or reflects is always short-lived and serves to set off something much less cosy. Chapter 6 ends with Frankenstein in an unusually buoyant mood: "A serene sky and verdant fields filled me with ecstacy. The present season was indeed divine; the flowers of spring bloomed in the hedges, while those of summer were already in bud" (p. 70). At the beginning of Chapter 7, Frankenstein learns that William has been murdered.

It is the sublime settings—the region around Mont Blanc and the Arctic wastelands—which predominate among the book's scenic effects. The history of the sublime as a philosophical category is lengthy and complicated. Of present concern is what may be termed the natural sublime as distinct from the earlier concept of a rhetorical sublime which consists of certain stylistic devices elaborated by Longinus. Marjorie Hope Nicolson provides an excellent account of the development of the natural sublime in *Mountain Gloom and Mountain Glory*.[2] She observes that while Longinus did regard the power of forming great conceptions as essential to the achievement of the sublime, it was not until the new astronomy and the new geology of the seventeenth century precipitated a new sense of the vastness of space and time that natural analogies were found for those sublime emotions previously associated directly with the deity. Mountains and oceans, once regarded as fallen disfigurements of the originally smooth surface of the mundane egg Earth, together with the reaches of interstellar space, were suddenly appreciated as evocative of the sublime emotions of terror and religious awe.

Thomas Burnet in his extraordinary *The Sacred Theory of the Earth* (1684) (a work which occupies a pivotal position in the aesthetic history of the sublime) touches on the three natural stimuli of the sublime in the following passage:

The greatest Objects of Nature are, methinks, the most pleasing to behold; and next to the Great Concave of the

Heavens, and those boundless regions where the Stars inhabit, there is nothing that I look upon with more Pleasure than the wide Sea and the Mountains of the Earth. There is something august and stately in the Air of these things, that inspires the Mind with great Thoughts and Passions; we do naturally, upon such Occasions, think of God and His greatness: And whatsoever hath but the Shadow and Appearance of INFINITE, as all things do have that are too big for our comprehension, they fill and overbear the Mind with their Excess, and cast it into a pleasing kind of Stupor and Admiration.[3]

Walton alludes to the same three "Objects" when he notes of Frankenstein that "The starry sky, the sea, and every sight afforded by these wonderful regions [the mountainous Arctic], seem still to have the power of elevating his soul from earth" (p. 29). Even the most casual reader of *Frankenstein* cannot fail to notice that a considerable portion of the book is given over to natural description, particularly of "the sublime shapes of the mountains" (p. 36) and tempestuous seas. The plot does not allow for any space voyages but that sublime region is at least implied by the repeated references to the moon. Robert M. Philmus undoubtedly speaks for many readers when he complains that the landscape in *Frankenstein* severely interrupts the development of the plot.[4] I hope to show that what Philmus regards as a negative feature is actually the source of the book's vitality. Towards this end it is important to appreciate that Mary Shelley chose to emphasize certain natural phenomena with an eye to evoking the natural sublime.

The qualities that constitute the sublime experience have been variously analysed. Joseph Addison in his *Pleasures of the Imagination* (1712) emphasizes the importance of the uncommon while Edmund Burke in *A Philosophical Enquiry into the Origin of our Ideas of the Sublime and Beautiful* (1757) stresses the value of obscurity because it excites fear of the unknown, specifically as related to the ideas of infinity and eternity. According to Burke, astonishment "is the effect of the sublime in its highest degree, but terror is the ruling principle of the sublime."[5] He claims that "the English *astonishment* and *amazement*, point out ... clearly the kindred emotions which attend fear and wonder."[6] But it is an awareness of the power implied by sublime phenomena which produces the emotion of terror and that "delightful horror, which is the most genuine effect and truest test of the sublime."[7]

Clearly, the sublime experience offered in *Frankenstein* has much in common with Burke's prescription. It is the powerful and terrifying aspects of mountains and seas which make the strongest impression. As for the moon, while it is not overtly powerful or terrifying (except for the reader conscious of the moon's influence on the tide), it gains those qualities by being consistently associated with the monster. By a light half-dead, "the half-extinguished light" of a candle, Frankenstein first observes the process of animation: "I saw the dull yellow eye of the creature open; it breathed hard, and a convulsive motion agitated its limbs" (p. 57). Frankenstein, asleep after taking to his bed in horror, awakens to further horror: "my teeth chattered, and every limb became convulsed: when, by the dim and yellow light of the moon, as it forced its way through the window shutters, I beheld the wretch—the miserable monster whom I had created" (p. 58). The equation between the monster and the moon is doubly confirmed. "The dull yellow eye" of the one is complemented by "the dim yellow light" of the other. Because of a syntactical ambiguity, it is unclear whether the moon's light or the "wretch" "forced its way through the window shutters." It should also be observed that the "convulsive motion" which agitated the monster's limbs is transferred to Frankenstein whose "every limb became convulsed." Here is further evidence that the monster is Frankenstein's double. But since the moon and the monster are identified, should the moon also be seen as a projection of Frankenstein's inner reality? The answer, as should be apparent from my previous argumentation and as will become increasingly clear during the balance of this book, is both yes and no.

Amidst the confused sensations that characterize the monster's initial moments of awareness, he observes "a radiant form rise from among the trees." This, "the only object that I could distinguish was the bright moon," and by its light, like Caliban, with "innumerable sounds" (p. 103) ringing in his ears, the monster goes in search of berries. Much later, Frankenstein in his Orkneys laboratory "saw by the light of the moon, the daemon at the casement" (p. 166). Shortly thereafter, while "hung over" the body of Elizabeth (as the monster twice hangs over his own body), Frankenstein "felt a kind of panic on seeing the pale yellow light of the moon illuminate the chamber" (p. 196). Frankenstein's associative processes do not play him false. Once again the monster is at the window. When Frankenstein next sees the monster, having sworn vengeance and been disturbed by a familiar voice at his ear, the same association applies: "Suddenly the broad disk of the moon arose, and shone full upon his ghastly and distorted shape as he fled with more than mortal speed" (p. 203).

I have documented the connection between the moon and the monster in order to show how the qualities of Burke's sublime, most obviously manifested in Mary Shelley's descriptions of mountains and raging seas, are also attached to the moon. But the qualities which the monster bestows on the moon he himself appears to gain from the Alpine environment. The monster is almost a projection of the sensations inspired by the book's Alpine setting, the same setting which so affected Thomas Burnet and many of the other testifiers to mountain glory. The monster is at least as much a creation of the mountainous setting as of Frankenstein's more constrained laboratory. To this extent it might be argued that the monster is a personification of Burke's natural sublime. Presumably, Sir Walter Scott, in the most perspicacious early review of *Frankenstein*, reacts to something similar about the monster when he notes "the mysterious sublimity annexed to his first appearance."[8]

The sense that the mountains, especially Mont Blanc, were somehow alive or the embodiment of a powerful spirit is one that Mary Shelley seems to have shared with, and perhaps derived from, her husband. Between July 21st and July 27th, 1816, the Shelleys (in the company of a maid and Claire) visited the area around the village of Chamonix which figures so prominently in *Frankenstein*. Mary's *Journal*, silent for the preceding months, contains a detailed description of the *Mer de Glace* and Mont Blanc, a description that dovetails perfectly with that in the Frankenstein episode she wrote two days after returning to the Villa Chapuis. But this episode also parallels Percy Shelley's reaction to the experience as recorded in a letter to Thomas Love Peacock and in the poem written shortly thereafter entitled "Mont Blanc." In the portion of a letter to Peacock written July 25, 1816, Shelley concluded "that Mont Blanc was a living being & that the frozen blood forever circulated slowly thro' his stony veins."[9] The treatments of Mont Blanc and the surrounding region in Shelley's poem and in *Frankenstein* convey the same sense of animism. The documentary evidence might seem to support an argument that Shelley influenced Mary. However, this sense of presence in nature and the corresponding philosophical perplexities regarding the perceiver's role in what may after all be an illusion, a mere pathetic fallacy, is Wordsworthian as well as Shelleyan, and I prefer to think that here Mary and Shelley were of one mind.

Notes

2. *Mountain Gloom and Mountain Glory: The Development of the Aesthetics of the Infinite* (Ithaca, N.Y.: Cornell University Press, 1959).

3. *The Sacred Theory of the Earth: Containing an Account of the Original of the Earth and of All the General Changes Which It Hath Already Undergone or Is to Undergo, till the Consummation of All Things* (London: Walter Kettilby, 1684). The quotation is taken from the sixth edition of 1726, I, 188–89.

4. *Into the Unknown: The Evolution of Science Fiction from Francis Godwin to H. G. Wells* (Berkeley: University of California Press, 1970), p. 84.

5. *A Philosophical Enquiry into the Origins of our Ideas of the Sublime and Beautiful*, ed. J. T. Boulton (London: Routledge & Paul, 1958), p. 57.

6. *Ibid.*, p. 58.

7. *Ibid.*, p. 73.

8. "Remarks on *Frankenstein* ...," 617–18.

9. *The Letters of Percy Bysshe Shelley*, ed. Frederick L. Jones (London: Oxford University Press, 1964), I, 500. Shelley's poetic reaction to

90

another mountain in 1818 is similarly anthropomorphic but also, I suspect, a deliberate and perhaps jocular literalization of an idea that is present only metaphorically in *Frankenstein*:

> Listen, listen Mary mine,
> To the whisper of the Apennine,
> ....
> The Apennine in the light of day
> Is a mighty mountain dim and grey
> Which between the earth and sky doth lay;
> But when the night comes, a chaos dread
> On the dim starlight then is spread
> And the Apennine walks abroad with the storm.

See "Passage to the Apennines" in *The Complete Works of Percy Bysshe Shelley*, ed. Roger Ingpen and Walter E. Peck (London: Ernest Benn Ltd., 1926–30), III, 199. A possible source for this fantasy in *Frankenstein* occurs in the context of the boat-stealing episode in *The Prelude*. Wordsworth writes:

>   a huge peak, black and huge
> As if with voluntary power instinct,
> Upreared its head. I struck and struck again
> And growing still in stature the grim shape
> Towered up between me and the stars, and still,
> For so it seemed, with purpose of its own
> And measurèd motion like a living thing,
> Strode after me. (I, 378–85)

Subsequently, Wordsworth records "unknown modes of being" (I, 393) and "huge and mighty forms that do not live / Like living men ... were a trouble, to my dreams" (I, 398–400).

MURIEL SPARK ON THE SHIFTING ROLES OF FRANKENSTEIN AND HIS MONSTER

There are two central figures—or rather two in one, for Frankenstein and his significantly unnamed Monster are bound together by the nature of their relationship. Frankenstein's plight resides in the Monster, and the Monster's in Frankenstein. That this fact has received wide, if unwitting, recognition is apparent from the common mistake of naming the Monster "Frankenstein" and emanates from the first principle of the story, that Frankenstein is perpetuated in the Monster. Several implicit themes show these characters as both complementary and antithetical beings.

The most obvious theme is that suggested by the title, *Frankenstein—Or, The Modern Prometheus*. (That casual, alternative *Or* is worth noting, for though at first Frankenstein is himself the Prometheus, the vital fire-endowing protagonist, the Monster, as soon as he is created, takes on the role. His solitary plight—"... but am I not alone, miserably alone?" he cries—and more especially his revolt against his creator establish his Promethean features. So, the title implies, the Monster is an alternative Frankenstein.)

The humanist symbol of Prometheus was one that occupied Shelley in many forms beside that of his *Prometheus Unbound*, and Shelley's influence on Mary had gained time to give figurative shape to Godwin's view of mankind's situation. It is curious that Shelley should have written in his Preface to *Frankenstein*:

The opinions which naturally spring from the character and situation of the hero are by no means to be conceived as existing always in my [that is, Mary's] own conviction; nor is any inference justly to be drawn from the following pages as prejudicing any philosophical doctrine of whatever kind.

Curious, because one cannot help inferring a philosophical attitude; but not so curious when we remember Shelley's refusal to admit the didactic element in his own poetry.

Less curious, however, is the epigraph to the book (original edition):

Did I request thee, Maker, from my clay
To mould me man? Did I solicit thee
From darkness to promote me?
   Paradise Lost

The motif of revolt against divine oppression, and indeed, against the concept of a benevolent deity, which is prominent in much of Shelley's thought, underlines the "Modern Prometheus" theme of *Frankenstein*. "You accuse me of murder," the Monster reproaches his maker, "and yet you would, with a satisfied conscience, destroy your own creature"—not the least of *Frankenstein's* echoes from Shelley.

The Prometheus myth is one of action but not of movement; that is, the main activity of the original story is located around the tortured Prometheus himself, chained to one spot. A novel, however, demands a certain range of activity, and in *Frankenstein* the action is released from its original compression by a secondary theme—that of pursuit, influenced most probably by Godwin's *Caleb Williams*. It is this theme that endows the novel, not only with movement, but with a pattern, easily discernible because it is a simple one.

It begins at Chapter V with the creation of the Monster who becomes, within the first two pages, Frankenstein's pursuer. He is removed for a time from the vicinity of his quarry, but continues to stalk the regions of Frankenstein's imagination, until it is discovered that he has been actually prosecuting his role through the murder of Frankenstein's young brother, William. Frankenstein is then hounded from his homeland to the remote reaches of the Orkney Islands where he is to propitiate his tormentor by creating a Monster-bride for him.

If we can visualise this pattern of pursuit as a sort of figure-of-eight macaberesque—executed by two partners moving with the virtuosity of skilled ice-skaters—we may see how the pattern takes shape in a movement of advance and retreat. Both partners are moving in opposite directions, yet one follows the other. At the crossing of the figure eight they all but collide. Such a crossing occurs when Frankenstein faces his Monster alone in the mountains, and another, when Frankenstein makes his critical decision to destroy his nearly completed female Monster. Once these crises are passed, however, we find Frankenstein and the Monster moving apparently away from each other, but still prosecuting the course of their pattern. It is not until Frankenstein, on his bridal night, finds his wife murdered by the Monster that the roles are reversed. Frankenstein (to keep our image) increases his speed of execution, and the Monster slows down; now, at Chapter XXIV, Frankenstein becomes the pursuer, the Monster, the pursued.

Thenceforward, this theme becomes the central focus of the story. Motives have already been established, and we are induced to forget them, since hunter and hunted alike find a mounting exhilaration in the chase across frozen Arctic wastes, until it becomes the sole *raison d'être* of both. Frankenstein is urged in his pursuit, and in fact sustained, by the Monster:

> Sometimes, indeed, he left marks in writing on the barks of the trees, or cut in stone, that guided me and instigated my fury. (...) "You will find near this place, if you follow not too tardily, a dead hare; eat and be refreshed. Come on, my enemy."

And one of the most memorable passages in the book occurs where the Monster again instructs his creator:

> "Wrap yourself in furs and provide food; for we shall soon enter upon a journey where your sufferings will satisfy my everlasting hatred."

I find that "wrap yourself in furs" very satisfying; as I do Frankenstein's rationalisation of his own fanatical relish in the chase; he swears:

> to pursue the daemon who caused this misery until he or I shall perish in mortal conflict. For this purpose I will preserve my life.

until he comes to conceive himself divinely appointed to the task, his purpose "assigned ... by Heaven."

The whole ironic turn of events is, I think, a stroke of genius. Mary's treatment of this theme alone elevates her book above *Caleb Williams* and other novels which deal with the straightforward hunter-and-hunted theme. By these means the figures retain their poise to the very end. No collision occurs, and the pattern is completed only by Frankenstein's natural death and the representation of the Monster hanging over him in grief. They merge one into the other, entwined in final submission.

The pattern of pursuit is the framework of the novel, a theme in itself which encloses a further theme; there, Frankenstein's relationship to the Monster expresses itself in the paradox of identity and conflict—an anticipation of the Jekyll-and-Hyde theme—from which certain symbolic situations emerge. Frankenstein himself states:

> I considered the being whom I had cast among mankind (...) nearly in the light of my own vampire, my own spirit let loose from the grave, and forced to destroy all that was dear to me.

We may visualise Frankenstein's doppelgänger or Monster firstly as representing reason in isolation, since he is the creature of an obsessional rational effort. The manifest change in Frankenstein's nature after the creation of the Monster can be explained by the part-separation of his intellect from his other integral properties. He becomes a sort of Hamlet figure, indecisive and remorseful too late. He decides to destroy the Monster, but is persuaded to pity him—he decides to make a female Monster, but fails at the last moment—he receives the Monster's threat of revenge and does nothing: "Why had I not followed him, and closed with him in mortal strife? But I had suffered him to depart," Frankenstein muses bitterly when the damage has been done. And he admits,

> through the whole period during which I was the slave of my creature, I allowed myself to be governed by the impulses of the moment.

After the Monster's "birth," then, Frankenstein is a disintegrated being—an embodiment of emotion and also of imagination minus intellect. When, in his final reflections, Frankenstein realises that it was not always so, and exclaims,

> My imagination was vivid, yet my powers of analysis and application were intense; by the union of these qualities I conceived the idea and executed the creation of a man.

he reminds us of those eighteenth-century geniuses (the story of Frankenstein is set in that century) whose too-perfect balance of imaginative and rational faculties did in fact so often disintegrate and ultimately destroy them.

Generally speaking, therefore, it is the emotional and the intellectual that conflict in the form of Frankenstein and his Monster. The culminating emotional frustration by the intellect is reached in the murder of Frankenstein's bride by the Monster. Thereafter, Frankenstein's hysterical pursuit of his fleeting reason completes the story of his madness—a condition perceived in the tale only by the Genevan magistrate, who, when Frankenstein demands of him the Monster's arrest, "endeavoured," says Frankenstein, "to soothe me as a nurse does a child."

Richard Church recognised a parallel in Mary Shelley's life when he discussed the murder of Frankenstein's brother, William. "At the time that she was writing this book," Mr. Church remarks, "the baby William was in the tenderest and most intimate stage of dependent infancy.... It is almost inconceivable that Mary could allow herself to introduce a baby boy into her book; deliberately call him William, describe him in terms identical with those in which she portrays her own child in one of her letters—and then let Frankenstein's monster waylay this innocent in a woodland dell and murder him by strangling."

Sandra M. Gilbert and Susan Gubar on Milton's Influence

Walton and his new friend Victor Frankenstein have considerably more in common than a Byronic (or Monk Lewis-ish) Satanism. For one thing, both are orphans, as

Frankenstein's monster is and as it turns out all the major and almost all the minor characters in *Frankenstein* are, from Caroline Beaufort and Elizabeth Lavenza to Justine, Felix, Agatha, and Safie. Victor Frankenstein has not always been an orphan, though, and Shelley devotes much space to an account of his family history. Family histories, in fact, especially those of orphans, appear to fascinate her, and wherever she can include one in the narrative she does so with an obsessiveness suggesting that through the disastrous tale of the child who becomes "an orphan and a beggar" she is once more recounting the story of the fall, the expulsion from paradise, and the confrontation of hell. For Milton's Adam and Eve, after all, began as motherless orphans reared (like Shelley herself) by a stern but kindly father-god, and ended as beggars rejected by God (as she was by *God*win when she eloped). Thus Caroline Beaufort's father dies leaving her "an orphan and a beggar," and Elizabeth Lavenza also becomes "an orphan and a beggar"— the phrase is repeated (18, 20, chap. 1)—with the disappearance of her father into an Austrian dungeon. And though both girls are rescued by Alphonse Frankenstein, Victor's father, the early alienation from the patriarchal chain-of-being signalled by their orphanhood prefigures the hellish fate in store for them and their family. Later, motherless Safie and fatherless Justine enact similarly ominous anxiety fantasies about the fall of woman into orphanhood and beggary.

Beyond their orphanhood, however, a universal sense of guilt links such diverse figures as Justine, Felix, and Elizabeth, just as it will eventually link Victor, Walton, and the monster. Justine, for instance, irrationally confesses to the murder of little William, though she knows perfectly well she is innocent. Even more irrationally, Elizabeth is reported by Alphonse Frankenstein to have exclaimed "Oh, God! I have murdered my darling child!" after her first sight of the corpse of little William (57, chap. 7). Victor, too, long before he knows that the monster is actually his brother's killer, decides that his "creature" has killed William and that therefore he, the creator, is the "true murderer": "the mere presence of the idea," he notes, is "an irresistable proof of the fact" (60, chap. 7).

Complicity in the murder of the child William is, it seems, another crucial component of the Original Sin shared by prominent members of the Frankenstein family.

At the same time, the likenesses among all these characters—the common alienation, the shared guilt, the orphanhood and beggary—imply relationships of redundance between them like the solipsistic relationships among artfully placed mirrors. What reinforces our sense of this hellish solipsism is the barely disguised incest at the heart of a number of the marriages and romances the novel describes. Most notably, Victor Frankenstein is slated to marry his "more than sister" Elizabeth Lavenza, whom he confesses to having always considered "a possession of my own" (21, chap. 1). But the mysterious Mrs. Saville, to whom Walton's letters are addressed, is apparently in some sense *his* more than sister, just as Caroline Beaufort was clearly a "more than" wife, in fact a daughter, to her father's friend Alphonse Frankenstein. Even relationless Justine appears to have a metaphorically incestuous relationship with the Frankensteins, since as their servant she becomes their possession and more than sister, while the female monster Victor half-constructs in Scotland will be a more than sister as well as a mate to the monster, since both have the same parent/creator.

Certainly at least some of this incest-obsession in *Frankenstein* is, as Ellen Moers remarks, the "standard" sensational matter of Romantic novels.[24] Some of it, too, even without the conventions of the gothic thriller, would be a natural subject for an impressionable young woman who had just spent several months in the company of the famously incestuous author of *Manfred*.[25] Nevertheless, the streak of incest that darkens *Frankenstein* probably owes as much to the book's Miltonic framework as it does to Mary Shelley's own life and times. In the Edenic cosiness of their childhood, for instance, Victor and Elizabeth are incestuous as Adam and Eve are, literally incestuous because they have the same creator, and figuratively so because Elizabeth is Victor's pretty plaything, the image of an angelic soul or "epipsyche" created from his own soul just as Eve is created from Adam's rib. Similarly, the incestuous relationships of Satan and Sin, and by implication of Satan and Eve, are mirrored in the incest fantasies of *Frankenstein*, including the disguised but intensely sexual waking dream in which Victor Frankenstein in effect couples with his monster by applying "the instruments of life" to its body and inducing a shudder of response (42, chap. 5). For Milton, and therefore for Mary Shelley, who was trying to understand Milton, incest was an inescapable metaphor for the solipsistic fever of self-awareness that Matthew Arnold was later to call "the dialogue of the mind with itself."[26]

If Victor Frankenstein can be likened to both Adam and Satan, however, who or what is he *really*? Here we are obliged to confront both the moral ambiguity and the symbolic slipperiness which are at the heart of all the characterizations in *Frankenstein*. In fact, it is probably these continual and complex reallocations of meaning, among characters whose histories echo and re-echo each other, that have been so bewildering to critics. Like figures in a dream, all the people in *Frankenstein* have different bodies and somehow, horribly, the same face, or worse—the same two faces. For this reason, as Muriel Spark notes, even the book's subtitle "The Modern Prometheus" is ambiguous, "for though at first Frankenstein is himself the Prometheus, the vital fire-endowing protagonist, the Monster, as soon as he is created, takes on [a different aspect of] the role."[27] Moreover, if we postulate that Mary Shelley is more concerned with Milton than she is with Aeschylus, the intertwining of meanings grows even more confusing, as the monster himself several times points out to Frankenstein, noting "I ought to be thy Adam, but I am rather the fallen angel," (84, chap. 10), then adding elsewhere that "God, in pity, made man beautiful ... after His own image; but my form is a filthy type of yours.... Satan had his companions ... but I am solitary and abhorred" (115, chap. 15). In other words, not only do Frankenstein and his monster both in one way or another enact the story of Prometheus, each is at one time or another like God (Victor as creator, the monster as his creator's "Master"), like Adam (Victor as innocent child, the monster as primordial "creature"), and like Satan (Victor as tormented overreacher, the monster as vengeful fiend).

What is the reason for this continual duplication and reduplication of roles? Most obviously, perhaps, the dreamlike shifting of fantasy figures from part to part, costume to costume, tells us that we are in fact dealing with the psychodrama or waking dream that Shelley herself suspected she had written. Beyond this, however, we would argue that the fluidity of the narrative's symbolic scheme reinforces in another way the crucial significance of the Miltonic skeleton around which Mary Shelley's hideous progeny took shape. For it becomes increasingly clear as one reads *Frankenstein* with *Paradise Lost* in mind that because the novel's author is such an inveterate student of literature, families, and sexuality, and because she is using her novel as a tool to help her make sense of her reading, *Frankenstein* is ultimately a mock *Paradise Lost* in which both Victor and his monster, together with a number of secondary characters, play all the neo-biblical parts over and over again—all except, it seems at first, the part of Eve. Not just the striking omission of any obvious Eve-figure from this "woman's book" about Milton, but also the barely concealed sexual components of the story as well as our earlier analysis of Milton's bogey should tell us, however, that for Mary Shelley the part of Eve is all the parts.

On the surface, Victor seems at first more Adamic than Satanic or Eve-like. His Edenic childhood is an interlude of prelapsarian innocence in which, like Adam, he is sheltered by his benevolent father as a sensitive plant might be "sheltered by the gardener, from every rougher wind" (19–20, chap. 1). When cherubic Elizabeth Lavenza joins the family, she seems as "heaven-sent" as Milton's Eve, as much Victor's "possession" as Adam's rib is Adam's. Moreover, though he is evidently forbidden almost nothing ("My parents [were not] tyrants ... but the agents and creators of many delights"), Victor hints to Walton that his deific father, like Adam's and Walton's, did on one occasion arbitrarily forbid him to pursue his interest in arcane knowledge. Indeed, like Eve and Satan, Victor blames his own fall at least in part on his father's apparent arbitrariness. "If ... my father had taken the pains to explain to me that the principles of Agrippa had been entirely exploded.... It is even possible that the train of my ideas would never have received the fatal impulse that led to my ruin" (24–25, chap. 2). And soon after asserting this he even associates an incident in which a tree is struck by Jovian thunder bolts with his feelings about his forbidden studies.

As his researches into the "secrets of nature" become more feverish, however, and as his ambition "to explore unknown powers" grows more intense, Victor begins to metamorphose from Adam to Satan, becoming "as Gods" in his capacity of "bestowing animation upon lifeless matter," laboring like a guilty artist to complete his false creation. Finally, in his conversations with Walton he echoes Milton's fallen angel, and Marlowe's, in his frequently reiterated confession that "I bore a hell within me which nothing could extinguish" (72, chap. 8). Indeed, as the "true murderer" of innocence, here cast in the form of the child William, Victor perceives himself as a diabolical creator whose mind has involuntarily "let loose" a monstrous and "filthy demon" in much the same way that Milton's Satan's swelled head produced Sin, the disgusting monster he "let loose" upon the world. Watching a "noble war in the sky" that seems almost like an intentional reminder that we are participating in a critical rearrangement of most of the elements of *Paradise Lost*, he explains that "I considered the being whom I had cast among mankind ... nearly in the light of my own vampire, my own spirit let loose from the grave and forced to destroy all that was dear to me" (61, chap. 7).

Notes

1. From Keats's annotations to *Paradise Lost*, quoted by Wittreich in *The Romantics on Milton*, p. 560.

2. George Eliot, *Middlemarch* (1871/1872; Cambridge, Mass.: Riverside Edition, 1956), book 1, chap. 7. All subsequent citations will be from this edition.

3. Letter to J. H. Reynolds, 17 April 1817, in *The Letters of John Keats*, ed. Hyder E. Rollins (Cambridge, Mass.: Harvard University Press, 1958), 1:130. See also Wittreich, p. 563, note 9.

4. *Middlemarch*, I, chap. 7.

5. Ibid.

6. Ibid., I, chap. 3.

7. Ibid.

8. Ibid.

9. Ibid. Interestingly; in deciding that Casaubon's work "would reconcile complex knowledge with devoted piety," Dorothea thinks at this point that "Here was something beyond the shallows of ladies'-school literature."

10. *A Room of One's Own*, p. 31.

11. Preface to *The World's Olio*, in *By a Woman writt*, ed. Joan Goulianos (Baltimore, Penguin Books, 1973), p. 60.

12. Anne Finch, "The Introduction," *Poems of Anne Countess of Winchilsea*.

13. From *Jane Anger her Protection for Women*, in Goulianos, p. 26.

14. See, for instance, Harold Bloom, "Afterword," *Frankenstein* (New York and Toronto: New American Library, 1965), p. 214.

15. Author's introduction to *Frankenstein* (1817; Toronto, New York, London: Bantam Pathfinder Edition, 1967), p. xi. Hereafter page references to this edition will follow quotations, and we will also include chapter references for those using other editions. For a basic discussion of the "family romance" of literature, see Harold Bloom, *The Anxiety of Influence*.

16. Robert Kiely, *The Romantic Novel in England* (Cambridge, Mass.: Harvard University Press, 1972), p. 161.

17. Moers, *Literary Women*, pp. 95–97.

18. See Ralph Wardle, *Mary Wollstonecraft* (Lincoln, Neb.: University of Nebraska Press, 1951), p. 322, for more detailed discussion of these attacks on Wollstonecraft.

19. Muriel Spark, *Child of Light* (Hodleigh, Essex: Tower Bridge Publications, 1951), p. 21.

20. See *Mary Shelley's Journal*, ed. Frederick L. Jones (Norman, Okla.: University of Oklahoma Press, 1947), esp. pp. 32–33, 47–49, 71–73, and 88–90, for the reading lists themselves. Besides reading Wollstonecraft's *Maria*, her *A Vindication of the Rights of Woman*, and three or four other books, together with Godwin's *Political Justice* and his *Caleb Williams*, Mary Shelley also read parodies and criticisms of her parents' works in these years, including a book she calls *Anti-Jacobin Poetry*, which may well have included that periodical's vicious attack on Wollstonecraft. To read, for her, was not just to read her family, but to read *about* her family.

21. Marc A. Rubenstein suggests that throughout the novel "the act of observation, passive in one sense, becomes covertly and symbolically active in another: the observed scene becomes an enclosing, even womb-like container in which a story is variously

developed, preserved, and passed on. Storytelling becomes a vicarious pregnancy." " 'My Accursed Origin': The Search for the Mother in *Frankenstein*," *Studies in Romanticism* 15, no. 2 (Spring 1976): 173.

22. See Anne Finch, "The Introduction," in *The Poems of Anna Countess of Winchilsea*, pp. 4–6, and Sylvia Plath, "The Moon and the Yew Tree," in *Ariel*, p. 41.

23. Speaking of the hyperborean metaphor in *Frankenstein*, Rubenstein argues that Walton (and Mary Shelley) seek "the fantasied mother locked within the ice ... the maternal Paradise beyond the frozen north," and asks us to consider the pun implicit in the later meeting of Frankenstein and his monster on the *mer* (or *Mère*) de Glace at Chamonix (Rubenstein " 'My Accursed Origin,' " pp. 175–76).

24. See Moers, *Literary Women*, pp. 99.

25. In that summer of 1816 Byron had in fact just fled England in an attempt to escape the repercussions of his scandalous affair with his half sister Augusta Leigh, the real-life "Astarte."

26. Matthew Arnold, "Preface" to *Poems*, 1853.

27. Spark, *Child of Light*, p. 134.

LAURA P. CLARIDGE ON FAMILIAL TENSIONS

The rights of kings are deduced in a direct line from the king of Kings, and that of parents from our first parent.

—Mary Wollstonecraft, *A Vindication of the Rights of Woman*

Everything must have a beginning.... And that beginning must be linked to something that went before.

—Mary Shelley, *Frankenstein*

Surely no one needs to be reminded that *Frankenstein* is a book largely reminiscent of Mary Shelley's own troubled family relationships; and in support of the point, one need only turn to George Levin and U. C. Knoepflmacher's excellent collection of essays, *The Endurance of Frankenstein*, to find the matter well documented.[1] That an author's life becomes translated into her fiction is hardly news on any account. But what has somehow eluded proper treatment is the resultant real subject of this "monster tale": the failure of human beings to "parent" their offspring in such a way that they will be able to take part in society rather than retreat into themselves.

An emphasis upon the proper assumption of parental responsibilities was part of the age: Maria Edgeworth and Hannah More had, through their educational treatises, influenced Walter Scott's Waverley themes, and Mary Shelley in turn bowed in his direction by allowing her husband to send him presentation volumes of *Frankenstein* the month the novel was published anonymously. The romantic educators typically placed the blame for an adolescent's misconduct at the door of a negligent (though often well-meaning) parent. Shelley herself subtly indicts Victor's parents in exactly this way; and she suggests an even subtler subtext of family conflict in the letters Walton writes to Margaret. Previous commentators have, of course, noted Frankenstein's abuse of his monster; strangely enough, however, they have tended to ignore the precedent within his own family for Victor's later actions, as well as the familial tensions that Walton, Victor's shadow self, implies. Such critical shortsightedness has inevitably resulted in textual analyses that fail to account for the complexity of this novel.

Readers have quite correctly assumed the statement in Shelley's preface, "my chief concern has been to exhibit the amiableness of domestic affection and the excellence of universal virtues" to be a cover-up; but in ascribing to Mary Shelley a need to deny the ugliness of a nightmarish vision they have missed her real subterfuge.[2] She will indeed concern herself with "domestic affection"—but more precisely, the lack of it, and how such a lack *undermines* "universal virtue."[3] In Shelley's attention to parent–child relationships, she implies a far-ranging application to society at large: if we fail at this most primal unit of communication, what hope is there for compassionate interaction within the larger community? Shelley insists that man can live only through communion with others; solitude, for her, represents death.

Through his continual exaggerations of familial love, Victor Frankenstein reveals to us the inadequacy of the homelife that belies his oft-fevered protestations of attachment. Perhaps the inevitable ambivalence concerning our own childhood creates a suspension of critical acuity in our reading Victor's story, but a close study of the text undercuts severely his insistence upon the perfect home. Critics have generally fallen for his defenses: Kate Ellis basically accepts his myth of the happy home;[4] Gubar and Gilbert call his childhood, in Miltonic terms, Edenic.[5] Only Christopher Small suggests that in Victor's description there is a "strained emphasis on felicity."[6]

That Victor insists upon remembering "the best of all possible worlds" is the psychological defense of an only child (as he was for a long time) who maintains a love/hate relationship with his parents because he senses that they share an affection that in some way excludes him.[7] Victor is an object of their love, not a participant in it; he is "their plaything and their idol" (p. 33). In his recollections of his parents' relationship—recollections more fully developed in the 1831 edition—he emphasizes their devotion to each other, to the (implicit) detriment of their child. If, as Victor claims, everything was centered on fulfilling the mother's wishes, one must wonder at the son's extravagant account of the love left over for him: "they seemed to draw inexhaustible stores of affection from a very mine of love to bestow them upon me" (p. 33). The narrator strains his credibility too far when he assures us that "every hour of my infant life I received a lesson of patience, of charity, and of self-control" (p. 34)—precisely those virtues that the young adult scientist will lack. After being told that "for a long time I was their only care," we are to believe that the addition of Elizabeth to his little family effected nothing but unqualified joy. There is no mention of the inevitable sibling friction; instead, these siblings were "strangers to any species of disunion or disrepute. Harmony was the soul of companionship ..." (p. 36). Frankenstein early on models upon his parents as Elizabeth becomes his plaything. His mother tells him, "I have a pretty present for my Victor—tomorrow he shall have *it*" (p. 35, emphasis mine). The child subsequently accepts Elizabeth as his "promised gift" and makes her his own possession.

We misread the story (and many have) if we listen to Victor's hyperbolic descriptions of a family idyll without attuning our ears to the subtext. When, for instance, Henry Clerval asks

Victor if they might talk "on an important subject" and Victor reacts with some anxiety, his friend quickly surmises that the scientist might be fearful to speak of his own home. Before proceeding, Clerval reassures his friend: "I will not mention it if it agitates you; but your father and cousin ... hardly know how ill you have been and are uneasy at your long silence" (p. 63). Victor responds: "How could you suppose that my first thought would not fly towards those dear, dear friends whom I love and who are so deserving of my love?" Both Clerval and the readers have some reason to doubt Victor's insistence. At this point in the narrative, he has not been home for five years; he will finally return home after yet another year passes, when he is summoned by his father upon William's death. Consequently, though he proclaims in frenzied terms that he loves his family "to adoration," we suspect that ambivalence, at the least, subverts his affection.

It is not only Victor who has troubled connections with his family; rather, we are in a world where parental irresponsibility and failure are the rule. Beaufort's pride puts his daughter in a difficult position; Safie's interests are betrayed by her father; Elizabeth is left an orphan; Justine's father dies and leaves his favorite at the mercy of a hard mother; and Henry Clerval's father attempts to keep him from the academic life he yearns to pursue. But more important than any family conflicts outside of the protagonist's is Walton's relationship to Margaret, that maternal sister who has apparently failed to be responsive to her younger brother's needs. He somewhat cynically reminds her, for instance, that of his efforts at poetry, she is "well acquainted with my failure and how heavily I bore the disappointment" (p. 17); and then, when discussing his latest venture, he implores: "And now, dear Margaret, do I not deserve to accomplish some great purpose? ... Oh, that some encouraging voice could answer in the affirmative!" (p. 17). Upon close reading we sense a compulsion on Walton's part to prove himself to Margaret; and if we ignore this underlying theme, as critics traditionally have done, we miss the emphasis in the novel on the murky undercurrents of what look at first glance to be straightforward parent–child relationships. In one sense, then, Victor's exaggerated (and therefore unmistakable) neglect of his progeny serves merely as a bolder-than-life projection of the novel's other, more oblique family conflicts. The parental failures are emblematic for those people unwilling to fulfill their duties to society at large: just as the hunter, that mythical image of a strong and protective father, reacts incorrectly and injures his charge's rescuer, so even the priestly fathers respond insensitively to their children's needs.[8] Justine's callous mother follows her confessor's advice in removing her daughter from the surrogate family where she is happy (p. 66); and when Justine is accused of murdering William, her priest helps condemn this innocent by threatening her into a false confession of guilt (p. 87). Even the De Laceys, who represent the family most at ease with itself, fail; De Lacey, a parent who is treated with the greatest deference and respect, responds compassionately to Frankenstein's child because he is blind and therefore not prejudiced by appearances. It is, ironically, when his sighted children return that the old man excludes the monster from a chance of kinship; it is when his children enable their father to "see through their eyes" that he loses his own visionary powers.

If, as Ellen Moers has suggested, "most of the novel—two of the three volumes, can be said to deal with the retribution visited upon the monster and creator for deficient infant care,"[9] it is also true that inadequate parental guidance in later years leaves its mark on Victor Frankenstein. The young scientist is thirteen, on the threshold of adolescence, when the struggle to break free of his parents and to become his own man begins in earnest. Not all fathers welcome their child's ascendant power, with its accompanying suggestion that their own is on the wane. Mary Shelley implicates this tension through her fascination with "the tale of the sinful founder of his race whose miserable doom it was to bestow the kiss of death on all the younger sons of his fated house, just when they reached the age of promise" (p. 7). She revised the second version of her novel to emphasize Victor's lack of guidance at this important formative stage; the first version allows the elder Frankenstein to share his son's interest in science, whereas in the second, Victor is left on his own.[10] In fact, when the exuberant youth tries to discuss his reading with his father, Alphonse Frankenstein carelessly glances at the title page and exclaims, "My dear Victor, do not waste your time upon this; it is sad trash" (p. 39). In one of Victor's rare insightful reflections, he explicitly criticizes his father's execution of his parental role: "If ... my father had taken the pains to explain to me [modern science] ... it is even possible that ... my ideas would never have received the fatal impulse that led to my ruin" (p. 39). Instead, he was abandoned "to struggle with a child's blindness ..." (p. 39). Finally, he is left mingling "a thousand contradictory theories and floundering desperately in a very slough of multifarious knowledge," guided by "childish reasoning" (p. 40).

Notes

1. U. C. Knoepflmacher, "Thoughts on the Aggression of Daughters," in *The Endurance of Frankenstein*, ed. George Levine and U. C. Knoepflmacher (Berkeley: Univ. of California Press, 1979), pp. 88–119, offers the most extensive treatment of the biographical soundings. See also Kate Ellis, "Monsters in the Garden: Mary Shelley and the Bourgeois Family" and Ellen Moers, "Female Gothic" in the same volume.

2. Mary Shelley, *Frankenstein*, ed. M. K. Joseph (London: Oxford Univ. Press, 1969), p. 14. All future citations will refer to this text. I realize, of course, that Percy Shelley wrote this preface, but Mary apparently agreed to the authorial explanation.

3. As is by now well known, Shelley had much to exorcise from her own family relationships. Her mother had died soon after childbirth. Her father, according to Christopher Small, "regarded infants as mere parcels, to be handed from one person to another without adverse effect" (*Mary Shelley's Frankenstein* [Pittsburgh: Univ. of Pittsburgh Press, 1972], p. 70). And we can easily associate the solipsistic Victor, whose sense of responsibility toward his creation is severely limited, with the Shelley who will, as Mary acknowledges, appreciate his child most "when he has a nursery to himself and only comes to you, just dressed and in good humor" (Frederick L. Jones, ed. *Mary Shelley's Journal* [Norman: Univ. of Oklahoma Press, 1947], p. 205; the entry occurs on 21 Oct. 1838).

4. Ellis in *The Endurance of Frankenstein*, p. 136.

5. Sandra M. Gilbert and Susan Gubar, "Horror's Twin: Mary Shelley's Monstrous Eve," in *The Madwoman in the Attic* (New Haven: Yale Univ. Press, 1979), p. 230.

6. Small, p. 73.
7. J. M. Hill, *"Frankenstein* and the Physiognomy of Desire," *American Imago*, 32, (1975), 346.
8. Bruno Bettelheim, *The Uses of Enchantment* (New York: Vintage Books, 1977), p. 205.
9. Moers, in *The Endurance of Frankenstein*, p. 81.
10. Ellis, in *The Endurance of Frankenstein*, p. 142.

BETTY T. BENNETT ON THE EXERCISE OF POWER AND RESPONSIBILITY

In *Frankenstein*, the exploration of power is played out on four different narrative-levels. First, the letters from the seafarer Robert Walton to his sister Margaret Walton Saville form the outer-frame for its particular story as well as for the other narratives. Second, the scientist Victor Frankenstein's telling of his version of the story of the history of his creation, abandonment, and death-struggle with the Creature. Third, the incorporation of the Creature's version of his abandonment, his desperate loneliness, and his transformation from goodness to evil as he mirrors his creator's values. And fourth, the Felix-Safie tale of heroism, injustice and love told within the Creature's story. To this, one might add a larger outer-frame: the unknown reader, escorted through Dantean circles of terror and pity, led on by the seductive attraction of reading letters addressed to someone else.

The interconnection of the levels by the delivery of the stories mirrors the likeness of the stories themselves: Walton, in his ambition to discover a new polar route, fantasizes about 'the inestimable benefit which I shall confer on all mankind to the last generation' (vol. 1, p. 4), thus acting out an applied, secular exploration, while Frankenstein's quest for the secret of life is on a metaphysical and theoretical scale. In the end, it is Walton who changes, placing the wishes of the community (the sailors on his ship) above his own ambitions. Felix's story is a series of injustices: a foreigner unjustly persecuted, a hero who saves him stripped of possessions and exiled, the foreigner in turn breaking his promise to allow Felix to marry his daughter, Safie. Although Safie defies her father by taking her jewels and joining her beloved, this tale ends in the injustice of Felix himself. When he sees the Creature, who has been secretly bringing food and firewood to the cottagers, rather than ask his story, as Felix's blind father does, he brutally attacks him, thus showing he, too, is a victim and promoter of the socio-political power structure. Moreover, the very form of the novel, story within story within story, iterates human interdependency, however accidental or unrecognized.

As in Dante's or Milton's epics which she drew on, the multiple layers of *Frankenstein* present a variety of visions but, unlike epic form, Mary Shelley presents no stable, reliable narrator. Instead, it is constantly left to the reader to evaluate the validity of a character's words and actions. In the end, we are given Frankenstein's loving father who nevertheless fails to properly educate his son; his mother who, in accordance with the social norms, abdicates all responsibility for the education of her son; Elizabeth, Frankenstein's fiancée, who also adheres to the social norms though she does undergo a change in which she loses first her faith in the justice system, and then her life, victimized directly and indirectly by Frankenstein's code; Clerval, a poet, murdered because of his best friend; Justine, a servant, forced to confess to a murder she didn't commit and then hanged for it; Frankenstein himself, a wealthy, indulged young man whose cognition of the norms of his society leads him to want, like a monarch or a God, absolute power and, whatever his disastrous experience, incapable of understanding his inherent error and accountability; and a very unheroic appearing Creature who goes from a state of natural goodness to one of crime and transgression, but fully understands and assumes responsibility for the horrors of his deeds, though incapable of restraining himself.

By subtitling her story 'The Modern Prometheus', Mary Shelley configures her story in the shadow of Prometheus' act of bringing light to humankind, concretizing the issue through examples of educational practices and their failure throughout the novel. But, in her purposive transformation of the older myth of enlightenment, with its expected benefit to humanity, she has created a new and dangerous story that challenges the rationale behind Victor Frankenstein's quest and his intended 'gift'. In the Prometheus myth, the result of his actions, like Christ's, is redemptive suffering for humanity. Frankenstein's quest conversely reveals itself to be more for the attainment of personal, god-like power than for societal advancement. In this reversal of expectation, Frankenstein becomes the first of a number of unheroic male central figures in Mary Shelley's fiction. A failed Prometheus, he suffers not for humankind, but for his own unprincipled judgment, and not willingly. This modern Prometheus, then, reduces the 'heroic' act to a mocking parody of enlightenment intention and execution.

The personification of that parody is the Creature, a Rousseauian natural savage who evolves from a condition of instinctual goodness to learned evil, mirroring a society based on fear, and more a bona fide member of that society than he ever realizes. Systems based on power are imbued with a fundamental expectation of danger and attack, which leads to a prevalent fear of the 'other'. The Creature, as constructed by Mary Shelley, is the living metaphor of that 'other', and as such expresses the position of any 'outsider' to the established authority. As the Creature educates himself first through contact with nature, then with Milton, Plutarch, Volney, and Goethe, and language itself, he is an argument for enlightenment theory as propounded by Godwin, Wollstonecraft, and the Shelleys. His innocence is destroyed by emulating the value system of power prevalent in the nineteenth century, the system perpetuated by his creator.

Frankenstein, then, may be seen as a republican form of the Prometheus myth. Power, in this telling, is in the hands of mortals who also have the capability of bringing light to civilization. The issue in *Frankenstein* is not, as in traditional religious arguments, a lesson in the dangers of the usurpation of God's domain. Rather, consistent with Mary Shelley's reformist ideology, the novel proposes that when either a Prometheus or a Frankenstein usurps power, it could be for good or evil. In questioning the very idea of power as an instrument of God, it suggests that unjust social conditions can be interpreted not as the work of God but rather of humanity itself, and therefore subject to change. Contemporary religious traditionalists were certainly aware of this implication, and a number of the reviews expressly addressed the issue. Suspicious of this Godwinian novel, they asserted that *Frankenstein* was a lesson in the dangers of attempting to usurp God's power or noted, within the same context, that it bordered on blasphemy (see vol. 1, introductory note).

Traditionalists have also applied the same conservative reading to the instruments of that implied usurpation: science and technology. But this obvious conclusion is inconsistent with the overall philosophy that informs *Frankenstein*, Mary Shelley's other works, and her comments in letters. It was science, from Copernicus and Galileo, incorporated into the theories of Newton, that shifted the understanding of the universe from a blend of the natural and supernatural, to the mechanistic vision that is at the very centre of enlightenment philosophy. If objects no longer have the essence of God in them, then any shape or essence is possible, and the search for that essence becomes a mechanism towards the creation of self-definition, individually and communally.

Both Shelleys saw scientific experimentation as a parallel with political experimentation: both offered the means to create a better world. Science was a major enthusiasm in England at the time, and P. B. Shelley's own strong interest in science[1] may have induced Mary Shelley, during the writing of *Frankenstein*, to read in the works of Sir Humphry Davy, a pioneer of galvanic electricity.[2] As the 1818 and 1831 introductions attest, P. B. Shelley's conversations with Lord Byron brought the evolutionary theories of Erasmus Darwin to Mary Shelley's attention.[3] But the theories of Darwin and Davy may have been familiar to her much earlier: both men were Godwin's friends.[4] Furthermore, it is possible that Mary Shelley may have had some tutelage in science generally through some of Godwin's many conversations with his admired friend William Nicholson, whom Godwin 'turned to for information on the latest theories in chemistry, physics, optics, biology, and other natural sciences'.[5] Rather than to be resisted, then, scientific exploration represented for Mary Shelley a ready contemporary paradigm for examining contemporary political inequities.

In this context, Frankenstein's limitation is not that he enters sacred realms but that he fails to take responsibility for his own actions. Akin to P. B. Shelley's *Alastor* (1816), who also delves in 'charnels and coffins' (l. 24)[6] and perishes a victim of self-centredness, Frankenstein fails to reach beyond himself. This defect is recognized by the Creature when he draws on his reading of *Paradise Lost* in comparing himself to Satan who wanted power for himself. The Creature's plea is one of many calls, unheard, to awaken Frankenstein: 'I ought to be thy Adam; but I am rather the fallen angel, whom thou drivest from joy for no misdeed [...] I was benevolent and good; misery made me a fiend. Make me happy and I shall again be virtuous.'[7]

But Frankenstein remains locked in his insular world, and the furies that beset this failed Prometheus are not suffered by him alone. His actions destroy the larger community, including his young brother William, Justine, Elizabeth, and Clerval. Frankenstein's failure, then, is a parable for the failure of the nineteenth-century socio-political structure to take responsibility—material and spiritual—for the greater populace. The novel iterates the Godwinian concept that a corrupt system will taint or destroy all its inhabitants, expressed in *Political Justice*, and then fictionalized in his novel *Caleb Williams*. *Frankenstein* resurrects these eighteenth-century societal theories in a model that offers its nineteenth-century audience, now shifted from revolutionary war to revolutionary commerce, the possibility of making responsible choices.

Frankenstein's choice in assembling and then responding to the Creature serves as a paradigm for individuals and societies as they newly assemble their society of their own 'component parts'. This is the connotation of the novel's epigraph, which raises the question of responsibility of both the creator and created:

Did I request thee, Maker, from my day
To mould me man? Did I solicit thee
From darkness to promote me?—
    (*Paradise Lost*, X. 743–5)

The characters of Frankenstein and the Creature, as well as their relationship, bring into question what and how we see; how we are conditioned to see; and, not least of all, how we create. The novel shifts the role of the artist-creator, Frankenstein's as well as Mary Shelley's, from observer and commentator, to shaper. *Frankenstein*, through its author, interpolates the woman as *the* creator, who comments on a failed sociopolitical system engineered and controlled by men. It also aligns her with visionary political reformers—among them, her parents and P. B. Shelley—who embraced the enlightenment belief in the potential improvement of humanity.

Notes
1. See, for example, Mary Shelley's manuscript that recounts Shelley's boyhood experiments with science, including 'a galvanic battery' and the 'charnel house' (Bodleian Library, MS. Shelley, adds. c. 5, f. 116); *PBSL*, I, pp. 227, 303.
2. *MWSJ*, I, pp. 142–4; see also Laura E. Crouch, 'Davy's *A Discourse, Introductory to A Course of Lectures on Chemistry*: A Possible Scientific Source for *Frankenstein*', *Keats-Shelley Journal*, Vol. XXVII (1978), pp. 35–44.
3. See *PBSL*, II, p. 472, for Shelley's reading in Davy and Darwin.
4. Brown, *William Godwin*, p. 128; David Knight, *Humphry Davy* (London: Blackwell, 1992), pp. 121–2.
5. St Clair, *Godwin*, p. 61; see note p. xvi, n. 6 above.
6. As Shelley actually had as a boy. See n. 1 above.
7. This edition, vol. 1, p. 74.

MATTHEW C. BRENNAN ON THE PSYCHOLOGY OF LANDSCAPE IN *FRANKENSTEIN*

"All Romantic horrors," Harold Bloom has said, "are diseases of excessive consciousness" (221). This remark may well explain why interpretations of Gothic novels are almost always psychological, and why in particular Mary Shelley's *Frankenstein* has accommodated such a variety of psychological approaches.[1] In fact, in the introduction she added to the revised 1831 edition, Mary Shelley seems to invite psychological and biographical approaches: "Invention," she writes, "it must be humbly admitted, does not consist in creating out of void, but out of chaos; the materials must, in the first place, be afforded" (8). As she began her novel at age 18, the most prominent materials in Shelley's consciousness (and unconscious) concerned conflicts stemming from the death of her mother, Mary Wollstonecraft, eleven days after giving birth to her second child—Mary. Following the critics who have dealt with this trauma, I intend to emphasize that *Frankenstein* is the result of her unresolved grief for her mother's death, a crisis she vitally needed to work through to forge her own adult identity.[2]

The psychological material most important to my approach here concerns Shelley's attitudes toward daydreams and landscape. What enabled her to endure the chaos of a motherless childhood, she implies in her introduction, was the indulgence in "waking dreams"; "they were," she says, "my refuge." Significantly, though she toured picturesque landscapes—landscapes William Gilpin prized for their external form and firm boundaries—Shelley stresses it was the "blank and dreary" landscapes that "fostered" her youthful flights of imagination. In other words, what produced her escape from an excessive consciousness of her sense of loss were sublime landscapes—landscapes which, in their vast, obscure shapelessness, allow for inner withdrawal from rational consciousness.[3]

Not surprisingly, therefore, as she begins her first novel, she writes of herself through the young adult Victor Frankenstein, who also faces the loss of his mother, Caroline, but never overcomes his grief, which is embodied by the Monster. Through this projection, Mary Shelley releases herself from the censorship the conscious mind places on painful memories and starts to work through her unresolved grief. In the novel these unresolved feelings parallel Victor's desire to resurrect the dead, as well as his longing to escape the Monster—and the grief it symbolizes—through three experiences of Nature:

the experience of the natural sublime that induces forgetfulness of sorrow; the experience of the natural sublime that both induces forgetfulness and contributes a comforting maternal power; and the experience of the maternal power of Nature apart from the sublime. Accordingly, after his mother's death, Victor can respond only to sublime and maternal landscapes, experiences of which provide his only escape from grief; in contrast, Henry Clerval, "the image of" his "former self," prefers the picturesque, which amuses the eye but doesn't alter consciousness. To show, then, how Mary Shelley uses landscape to symbolize Victor's regressive and gradually self-destructive response to grief, I want first to explain the preference of Victor's "former self"—his healthy childhood self—for the picturesque; and then to explain his later attraction, after his mother's death, to the sublime—an attraction that Shelley shared but transcended.

I

To enable us to grasp the violence of Victor's grief at his mother's death, Mary Shelley carefully sketches the domestic stability of his childhood. Victor's parents created so favorable an environment for Victor's early psychological development that he tells the Arctic explorer Robert Walton—on whose ship Victor narrates his part of the story—"No human being could have passed a happier childhood than myself" (37). Similarly, Victor remarks on the "exquisite pleasure" he feels "in dwelling on the recollections of childhood" (38). Among his first memories are images of his "mother's tender caresses" (33); and in fact this "mine of love" bestowed upon Victor was so "inexhaustible" that he felt like an "idol" (33): "I was so guided by a silken cord," he imagines, "that all seemed but one train of enjoyment" (34).

"Guided" is an especially apt verb, for his infancy was spent in picturesque rambles through Italy, France, and Germany (33). Because the picturesque typically involves travel with a guide, tutor, artist, or all three, it is an inherently more social mode of landscape appreciation than the sublime, which depends more on solitude. Furthermore, because the aesthetics of the picturesque stress line, form, and other surface qualities, its landscapes do not lead beyond themselves; they encourage attention to reality, not escape from it. So, by associating Victor's childhood with family tours of scenic landscape, Shelley establishes a psychological harmony that parallels the formal harmony of the picturesque. Later in the novel, she returns to this expressiveness of picturesque landscapes to indicate how far Victor has regressed in his grief from his former self, personified by his boyhood friend, Henry Clerval.

As Victor describes the tour he and Henry took through the Rhine valley after the death of his mother and the creation of the Monster, Victor himself remarks on "how great was the contrast between us" (154): for, unlike the solipsistic Victor who prefers the sublime of Switzerland and who abhors society (159), Clerval, being better balanced and more sociable, prefers the more social landscape of the Rhine—a landscape Victor categorizes as picturesque (155). Like William Gilpin in his *Tour of the Wye* (1782), Henry keeps a journal during the trip— a travelogue that records all the picturesque views and qualities in the landscape of the river valley. For instance, like Gilpin in the Wye valley, Henry finds the Rhine valley most picturesque when "the river descends rapidly and winds between hills, not high, but steep, and of beautiful forms" (155).

(...)

II

If Clerval is well suited to enjoy the surface charms of the picturesque, Victor, in contrast, is incapable of enjoying the picturesque because he cannot endure external reality. At Oxford, for instance, Victor notes that the colleges are picturesque, but his "enjoyment was embittered" by thoughts of the past (160). Indeed, throughout his picturesque travels in England and the Rhine valley, Victor's consciousness of present reality is tainted, for, as we eventually learn, the Monster has been shadowing him: ever hovering on the threshold of Victor's consciousness, the Monster constantly threatens to obtrude onto the picturesque landscape, thus forcing Victor to face the hideous reality he desires to escape. Clearly, then, the Monster manifests what Victor wants to suppress from consciousness. David Ketterer suggests that the Monster personifies the natural sublime (70), and in fact the Monster appears several times in the savage landscapes of the Alps and the Arctic. But however plausible this view may be, I believe, rather, that the Monster represents what Victor needs to forget—primarily, the fact of his mother's death—and that Victor resorts to the sublime to escape facing the Monster.

So, if the Monster does not personify the sublime, how, then, does Mary Shelley link the Monster with what Victor needs to repress through the sublime? First, not only does she emphasize Victor's idyllic and beneficent childhood, as we've seen; she also reintroduces Victor's childhood alchemical interest in animating the dead almost immediately after Caroline's death—"that most irreparable evil" (43)—and magnifies this interest into an obsession just when the plot's action begins to complicate and to rise. Critically, rather than continue his social development by marrying Elizabeth—the mate provided by his parents—and by creating with her a new generation, Victor instead regresses from the demands of adulthood: his sole motivation becomes the infantile desire to animate the dead.

Mary Shelley herself had fantasies of resurrecting the dead. After her first, nameless infant died, she dreamed of animating it. Significantly, as U. C. Knoepflmacher remarks, not only does Shelley's fantasy parallel Victor's, the fantasy that underlies *Frankenstein*; but "it could hardly have been Mary Shelley's first wishful 'dream' of making the dead come alive" (96)—which suggests she may well have dreamed of resurrecting her mother. In fact, in March 1817 while still at work on the novel, she explains an abrupt end to a letter to Leigh Hunt by stating, "I had a dream tonight of the dead being alive which has affected my spirits" (*Letters* 1:32). In her note to this dream, editor Betty T. Bennett argues that "the dead" could refer to Mary Wollstonecraft (*Letters* 1:33n).

(...)

III

In contrast to Byron's Childe Harold who fails to forget his sorrows in the Alpine landscape, Victor receives "the greatest consolation" from the "sublime and magnificent scenes" of the Alps (96): "They elevated me from all littleness of feeling, and although they did not remove my grief, they subdued and tranquilized it. In some degree, also, they diverted my mind from the thoughts over which it had brooded for the last month" (96). In particular, while gazing on the "awful majesty" of Mont Blanc, Victor's "heart, which was before sorrowful, now swelled with something like joy" (98). Similarly, in noting Victor's "constant and deep grief" (27), Walton says, "no one can feel more deeply than [Victor] does the beauties of nature"; he suffers "misery," Walton adds, "yet when he has retired into himself," it is as if he is encircled by a halo that no grief can penetrate (29).

But Victor's sublime withdrawal from external reality not only blots out thoughts of his mother's death; sometimes, this sublime consolation of forgetfulness also provides, through the maternal power of Nature, a second experience—a symbolic reunion with the lost mother. For example, while still in the Alps, Victor explains, "a tingling long-lost sense of pleasure often came across me during this journey" and "reminded me of days gone by, and were associated with the light-hearted gaiety of boyhood" (95), a time when his mother still lived. What produces these feelings of childhood are the maternal qualities of Nature: Nature is "kindly," the winds are "soothing," and the Arve makes "lulling sounds" that act "as a lullaby" bringing Victor the forgetfulness of sleep (95). As in Wordsworth's poetry, here the sublime provides both an escape from consciousness of the monstrous death of the mother and a return to her nurture through maternal Nature.

Notes

1. Several psychoanalytic studies have focused on Victor's character. For example, see Morton Kaplan and Gordon D. Hirsch. More helpful to my approach are studies that include biographical material. Ellen Moers discusses Mary's dark thoughts about teenage pregnancy, and Marc A. Rubenstein explores the effects on Mary of her mother's and

her first daughter's deaths. U. C. Knoepflmacher similarly considers Mary's relation to her mother, but in contrast to my argument stresses the lack of nurture she received from her stepmother as well as her ambivalence toward William Godwin, her father.

2. Clearly, Mary had a melancholy nature, which often focused on her mother: we know that before eloping with Percy Shelley she often spent afternoons at her mother's grave and suffered from an especially acute depression at age 15; and after eloping, in the relatively calm spring of 1816—just before the summer spent with Percy and Byron in Switzerland where she began her novel—she again suffered from depression. Moreover, in December 1816, when she finished "the 4 chap of Frankenstein," we know that her mother was on her mind, for she was reading her mother's book *A Vindication of the Rights of Woman*. See Scott. But as she began to write *Frankenstein*, Rubenstein says, "She was in a position of sufficient strength and tranquility to complete ... some of the postponed psychic work of adolescent development. In particular, she was coming to terms with her conflicted identification with the fantasy of her dead mother" (187). In fact, Shelley's "Author's Introduction" of 1831 connects her writing of the novel with the diminishment of grief: the novel, she writes, "was the offspring of happy days, when death and grief were but words which found no true echo in my heart" (10).

3. Though no critics have considered in depth the psychological implications of both the picturesque and the sublime in *Frankenstein*, David Ketterer discusses the presence in the novel of these 18th-century modes of landscape. Using a feminist approach, Fred V. Randel argues that the novel "exuberantly" criticizes "the infantilism latent in supernaturalism or sublime awe and passivity."

WILLIAM CRISMAN ON SIBLING RIVALRY

Sibling rivalry receives short mention (Claridge 16), but it never gains center stage as a way to read this novel. The neglect is strange on two grounds. First, sibling rivalry has as much place as "anti-oedipal" experiences and sad motherhood in Mary's childhood and teenage experience. She was "jealous" of the "abounding health and vivacity" of her half sister, Claire,[19] and acted with "muted hostility" toward her half brother (Knoepflmacher 103). Second, the novel focuses so plainly on the murder of siblings and near siblings that a reader would naturally wonder if sibling rivalry plays a prime role in the horrific plot.

The analysis that follows will make an assumption so old in *Frankenstein* criticism that it no longer needs extensive proof: that Victor's "creature" functions also as "his own Doppelgänger, his alter ego, his objectified id";[20] "it is customary by now to discuss Frankenstein and the monster as the feuding halves of a single personality" (Knoepflmacher 109), and most critics agree that "the monster's ugliness symbolizes his creator's own monstrosity."[21] Victor calls himself "creature" at a time long before *the* creature's production (29); calls himself directly "murderer" on several occasions (84, 88, and passim); and sometimes even dramatically appears like the creature, as when Victor portrays both of them bearing numerous pistols (189 and 204). That the murders are also Victor's murders, by his own admission, will be treated as a given. What is up for investigation is how much sibling rivalry functions as the motive.

Victor is an ideal candidate for sibling rival. Until the birth of Ernest he "remained for several years his [parents'] only child" in a situation where, he recalls, "no creature could have had more tender parents" (29). This quality of "tender" parent–child relations noticeably appears as well in the girlhood of Victor's mother, always an only child, a childhood which Victor imagines as one of "the greatest tenderness" (28). Mary Shelley expands on this situation in the 1831 edition, where Victor feels himself his parents' "idol," to whom they perform "duties ... owed" to him as a gift from "Heaven" (234). The appreciated tenderness toward the only child produces a megalomanic feeling that his existence is a divine gift to which worship is due.

From this position of imagined, ideal tenderness, Victor is brought into a situation of multiple siblings, a condition that may even seem plotted before his birth. Victor's father only considers marriage to have several "sons ... who might carry his name down to posterity" (27), even though Victor imagines himself in the singular as "the destined successor" (29).

Such a shock to the young "idol" "destined" to receive adorational "duties" is one that Victor tries to suppress in his oft-quoted remarks about his "perfect family," where life "passed happily," and "discontent never visited my mind" (37, 31, and 158). With Matthew Brennan as a rare exception,[22] most readers of the 1818 edition already take this idyllic description as suspiciously overstated, and Shelley in the 1831 edition gives the reader a direct glimpse behind the suppression in Victor's reference to his youthful "temper ... sometimes violent, and my passions vehement" (237).

The same edition emphasizes that such a violence arising from wanting to be an only child has been ingrained in Victor's general impressions. The mountain wanderings after William's death are ones "associated with ... boyhood" (248) in a location where nature has two child-related characteristics. On the one hand, the mountains "congregated round me ... they all gathered round me, and bade me be at peace" (249), suggesting "a reunion with the lost mother."[23] This twice-stated image of the single "me" encircled by adoring, huge shapes parallels a child's impression of being surrounded by much larger parents and draws out as well the megalomanic, Christ-child implication already present in Victor's sense of himself as Heaven's gift. On the other hand, the mountainous terrain also recalls a situation "ever and anon rent and torn, as if ... a plaything" (248 f.). Destruction of toys—the violence of the nursery—is the alternative to worship of the single child.

These impressions, especially drawn out in the 1831 edition, are already latent in 1818. Victor wants to be alone with "his" mountains. Already in the earlier version he "determined to go [the mountain route] alone, for ... the presence of another would destroy the solitary grandeur of the scene" (92). Again seeking to be in the center, he would boat alone "into the middle of [Lake Geneva]" and "gave way" to his "own ... reflections," "reflection" as often (especially on water) suggesting both thought and a narcissistic, visual self-mirroring. He is content as "the only ... thing ... in a scene so beautiful and heavenly." As he leaves the "middle" of this "heavenly" isolation, however, and approaches its periphery, a multiplicity of beings affront his senses, "some bat, or the frogs, whose harsh and interrupted croaking was heard only when I approached the shore" (86 f.). Leaving central isolation is to confront conventionally slimy creatures. The link between these loathesome things and siblings is not stretched. Swiss lakes are once again the nursery, where waves resemble "the play of a lively infant" (162), but violence usually appears in multiples. A "storm," Victor says, "as is often the case in Switzerland, appeared at once in various parts of the heaven" (71). The "lightnings" are also portrayed as "playing ... in the most beautiful figures," but with a "violence [that] quickly increased" (70). As symbolic nursery, Swiss lakes present two forms of alternative "play," the "lively" play of the single child, and the "violent" play of multiple figures that appear "at once."

Transferring this automatic way of perceiving non-human nature to Victor's way of perceiving human interchange is straightforward. As he wants to be the single, central figure on the lake, so Victor instinctively wants to be the single, central figure of the human realm. As the narrator, Walton, writes, Victor "seems to feel his own worth" (208). When in the 1831 edition Victor thinks of humankind in general, he blurts that he "abhorred the face of man. Oh, not abhorred! they were my brethren" (255). Even his casually conventional and general siblings, the "brethren" of humankind, evoke an instant "abhorrence" to be quickly suppressed, just as Victor's "passions violent" in childhood become suppressed behind the fiction of the "perfect family." The reader can chart the same suppressed abhorrence lexically in the shift between Victor's 1818 reference to "my fellow-creatures" to its 1831 version of "the beings of my own species" (259). "Fellow"ship is gone, replaced by a coldly grudging acknowledgment of biological kinship that implicitly rejects any other human bond. The reader might recall the bats and croaking frogs on the periphery of Victor's otherwise isolated lake.

In a transferred sense, Victor's destruction of the female creature comes from his awareness that she might bear a family of multiple "children, and a race of devils would be propagated upon the earth" (163). When he thinks of a childless union, before and after the partial assembly of the female creature,

Victor feels sympathy for the male creature (142 f. and 214). Importantly, when he imagines a truly monstrous family, he bypasses the otherwise harmonious possibility of a single baby and instantly leaps to a crowd of destructive "devils." Given this "abhorrence" of others and centering of the self, the murder of Victor's true sibling William makes perfect sense. Victor judges the baby William "the most beautiful little fellow in the world" (36), initiating a theme of physical beauty that will be important throughout. In near homoerotic appreciation, Walton will later praise Victor himself for "his fine and lovely eyes" (207). Victor is something of an acknowledged "beauty," and for his first impression of William to be that of "the most beautiful" already prepares for jealousy. Elizabeth's later reference to William's beauty as located in his "sweet laughing blue eyes" (62) makes the beauty contest with Victor's "lovely eyes" direct.

Furthermore, William inspires "the tenderest affection" (37). In its previous occurrences, "tender" is associated with the state of the single child, both Victor himself and his mother as a child. For Victor to apply the word to William suggests Victor feels his brother is being treated as if single, that is, as if Victor did not exist.

The reader learns also that William's portrait hangs, apparently alone, beneath that of their mother, a painting especially commissioned by their father. Visually the impression of William as only child has been built even into the interior design of the house. Significantly, what the mother's portrait depicts is her kneeling over the coffin of her father, a celebration of an always-only child's devotion. As Victor sees her portrait, he unconsciously refers to her by her maiden name, "Caroline Beaufort," indicating his awareness of the parent–single child relation (73).

When the creature, as Victor's alter ego, actually murders William, the elements of beauty competition and jealousy over parents come together. The creature is, of course, ugly in comparison with those around him; noticeably the "disgust and affright" this ugliness would inspire is specifically contrasted with Victor's beautiful mother as the creature sees her in William's locket. William more than anyone else in a short space reminds him of his deformity: " 'monster! ugly wretch!

... You are an ogre.... Hideous monster!'" Simultaneously William reminds the creature of paternal preference: "'I will tell my papa.... My papa ... would punish you'" (139). The single-child possessiveness of "my papa" is noticeable, and the murder of the "most beautiful" in the painted presence of the beautiful mother by the exaggeratedly and self-consciously ugly creature brings the reader back to the nursery of "rent and torn playthings" and "temper violent." Bringing the "misery home" to Mary Shelley, Ulrich Knoepflmacher reminds that Mary's own troublesome half brother was a "William" and Mary Thornburg's impression of sibling violence is so strong that she argues, oversubtly, that no "objective monster" was responsible for William's murder at all. Rather, Victor slipped out to commit the murder personally (Thornburg 86).

Notes

19. Lund, "Mary Shelley and the Monster" 256. Judith Weissman records Mary's happy letter on her half-sister's death, perhaps paralleling Victor's elation after William's death. "A Reading of *Frankenstein* as the Complaint of a Political Wife," *Colby Library Quarterly* 12 (1976): 174.

20. Lowry Nelson, Jr., "Night Thoughts on the Gothic Novel," *Yale Review* 52 (1963): 244. For an iteration of the Doppelgänger vocabulary, see Kaplan and Kloss, *Unspoken Motive* 139.

21. Tang Soo Ping, "*Frankenstein*, *Paradise Lost*, and the 'Majesty of Goodness,'" *College Literature* 16 (1989): 258; cf. M. A. Goldberg, "Moral and Myth in Mary Shelley's *Frankenstein*," *Keats-Shelley Journal* 8 (1959): 35; Kranzler, "Frankenstein and Technological Future" 43; Thornburg, *Monster in the Mirror* 6, 8, and 85; Kiely, *Romantic Novel in England* 165; and Masao Miyoshi, *The Divided Self: A Perspective on the Literature of the Victorians* (New York: New York UP, 1969) 83 f. George Levine says it is a "commonplace ... that the hero and his antagonist are one" ("*Frankenstein* and the Tradition of Realism," *Novel* 7 [1973]: 18). For a rare exception, see Burton R. Pollin, "Philosophical and Literary Sources of *Frankenstein*," *Comparative Literature* 17 (1965): 105, n. 27.

22. Matthew C. Brennan, "The Landscape of Grief in Mary Shelley's *Frankenstein*," *Studies in the Humanities* 15 (1988): 34.

23. Brennan, "Landscape of Grief," 39. Rubenstein discusses the importance of "centers" in the novel, "'My Accursed Origin'" 172 f. Milton Millhauser notes the extent to which the creature of Victor's making is both infant and adult at the same time. "The Noble Savage in Mary Shelley's *Frankenstein*," *Notes and Queries* 190 (1946): 249.

For self-centeredness and narcissistic reflection, see P. D. Fleck, "Mary Shelley's Notes to Shelley's Poems and *Frankenstein*," *SiR* 6 (1967): 249. The best study of mountains as symbols of parents is Fred V. Randel's "*Frankenstein*, Feminism, and the Intertextuality of Mountains," *SiR* 23 (1984): esp. 525.

JANIS MCLARREN CALDWELL ON SYMPATHY AND SIMILITUDE

SYMPATHY

Over the last few decades, the field of biomedical ethics has claimed *Frankenstein* as its classic narrative, a cautionary tale warning that science divorced from ethics will produce monsters. But *Frankenstein* is a critique not so much of an amoral science, as of a conflation of scientific and moral theory—in the theory of physiologic sympathy. In *Frankenstein*'s strange world, both scientifically modern and Gothically melodramatic, everybody is searching for sympathy, which functions as both a natural, material principle and the highest ideal of social interaction. The theory of physiologic sympathy, however, posits fragile bodies, susceptible to contagion and collapse. Under this model, social sympathy is safe only for people of nearly identical psychological and somatic constitutions. In *Frankenstein*, Shelley critiques the attempt to resolve science and ethics into a theory of physiologic sympathy, which she depicts as a narcissistic reduction, impatiently and prematurely synthetic in its demand for universal similitude, harmony, and unity.

Sympathy, judging from the word's frequency and weight in the text of *Frankenstein*, is the major theme and recurrent problem of the novel. Each narrator yearns for or mourns the loss of sympathetic relationship. Walton desires "the company of a man who could sympathize with me," and hopes he has found such a man when, with Frankenstein's arrival, the stranger's "constant and deep grief fills me with sympathy and compassion" (F, 13; F, 22). Walton's sympathy, however, is repulsed: "I thank you," Frankenstein replies,

126

"for your sympathy, but it is useless" (F, 24). Frankenstein has already had such a friend in Clerval, whose "true sympathy" is now destroyed (F, 69). As for the monster, who claims he "was fashioned to be susceptible of love and sympathy," he "sympathizes" with the DeLaceys as he witnesses how they "sympathized with one another" (F, 217; F, 108; F, 127). After his unsuccessful self-exposure to the DeLaceys, the failure of hoped-for sympathy tortures him: "Finding myself unsympathized with, [I] wished to tear up the trees, spread havoc and destruction around me, and then to have sat down and enjoyed the ruin" (F, 132). The monster then pursues Frankenstein with the demand that he create a female monster, thinking he cannot live without the "interchange of those sympathies necessary for my being" (F, 140). Frankenstein, although finally coerced into agreement, flatly states "I could not sympathize with him" (F, 143). And after Frankenstein's death, the monster concludes: "No sympathy may I ever find ... I am quite alone" (F, 218; F, 219). The search for sympathy amounts to an obsession for each narrator in this novel, and Shelley seems to be repeating that sympathy between individuals is impossible—or at least that it is a good deal more fragile than many Romantics assumed.[12]

For Shelley's generation, sympathy meant primarily fellow feeling—or, in David Marshall's definition, "the capacity to feel the sentiments of someone else."[13] But the word carried with it two other important historical connotations: of magical correspondence and of "modern" mechanical communication. Before the scientific revolution, sympathy implied powerful occult consonance that could occur on a variety of levels: celestial, between heavenly bodies; social, especially between friends, lovers, and relatives; physiological, between one's parts or organs, especially between mind and body, and elemental, between inanimate particles. For instance, in its oldest usage, sympathy was said to exist between the moon and the ocean, two lovers even at extreme distance, the liver and the mind, iron and a lodestone, and so on.[14] It seems that when correspondences were noted but unaccounted for—i.e., there was no clearly

detailed or adequately understood mode of communication—
sympathy became the explanatory concept.

In the eighteenth century, as physical science gained
authority, mechanical explanations were offered for sympathy,
and a crude materialism began to stand in for the previously
occult attributes of sympathy.

(...)

THE TEXT OF *FRANKENSTEIN*

Moving between ghost stories and scientific research, and
insisting on the validity of both Romantic and materialist
points of view, Mary Shelley follows the same vein of Romantic
materialism suggested by Hazlitt and by Keats. Her critique
targets the variety of ideas about sympathy that relied on the
insistent resemblance or identification, magically wrought,
materially necessary, or egotistically imagined, between
sympathetic participants. The problem with this kind of
sympathy, according to Mary Shelley, was that it presupposed
sameness and/or passivity as the necessary medium for such
communication, and, as a corollary, an easy permeability
between bodies and minds, and between people.

In good Gothic form, Shelley uses repetition of structure,
doubling of characters, and suggestions of incest to evoke the
fear of excessive similitude. The symmetries of *Frankenstein*
contribute to a suffocating sensation of enclosure in the novel.
The famous "frame" or "box-within-a-box" structure of
the novel, with Walton's letters to Mrs. Saville surrounding
Frankenstein's narration, which in turn surrounds the monster's
autobiography, gives this novel about monstrosity a perverse
neatness. Of course, there is the well-known doppelgänger
effect of Frankenstein and his creature, pursuing and pursued
by one another, exchanging the roles of master and servant.
Similarly, if less overtly, Walton is included in this brotherhood,
as each man's rhetoric resembles the others'. Each recounts his
story in the same vocabulary and lofty, oratorical style so that,
as Beth Newman writes, each narration is less a contrasting
point of view than an echoic parallel.[36]

The theme of excessive similitude recurs in the incestuous suggestions regarding the Frankenstein family. Caroline Beaufort is the ward of Victor's father for two years before he marries her. Elizabeth and Victor in the 1818 edition are cousins, and, to Victor, she is his "more than sister." When Victor seems reluctant to marry Elizabeth, Victor's father suspects that Victor views her as a sister, and Elizabeth asks, "But as brother and sister often entertain a lively affection towards each other, without desiring a more intimate union, may not such also be our case?" As a whole, the Frankenstein family is itself a "circle" with all undesirable things "banished" from its enclosure:

> Such was our domestic circle, from which care and pain seemed for ever banished. My father directed our studies, and my mother partook of our enjoyments. Neither of us possessed the slightest pre-eminence over the other; the voice of command was never heard amongst us; but mutual affection engaged us all to comply with and obey the slightest desire of each other. (F, 37)

The family's peace and equality is overshadowed by the perfection that prescribes a stultifying harmony, in which each member must "comply" and "obey."

Outside the family circle, each character searches for a reflection of himself, or, seen another way, for the engulfment or ownership of another. Walton desires a friend "whose eyes would reply to mine," wishes to "possess" the stranger Frankenstein "as the brother of my heart," and turns in his failure to seeking the sympathy of his sister, Mrs. Saville (F, 13; F, 22). Frankenstein's desire to create a species of his own stems from a desire for a relationship even closer, less diluted, than fatherhood:

> A new species would bless me as its creator and source; many happy and excellent natures would owe their being to me. No father could claim the gratitude of his child so completely as I should deserve their's [sic]. (F, 49)

And, of course, the monster wants a partner just like himself, created by the same "father": "My companion must be of the same species," he warns Frankenstein, "and have the same defects" (F, 140). Frankenstein incorporates this harmonic ideal into his search for knowledge. Shelley carefully details young Victor's early education, that "train of ideas" imparting "the fatal impulse that led to my ruin" (F, 33). Onto his son's occult reading of Cornelius Agrippa, Paracelsus, and Albertus Magnus, Victor's father superimposes corrective instruction in "modern" science. But modern science does not completely supplant alchemical pseudoscience, despite his father's practical lessons in electricity. Significantly, "by some fatality" (which Frankenstein alternately explains as resistance to paternal authority, disinclination for modern studies, and the "accident" of missing a lecture series), Victor arrives at the university well-versed only in the ancients. There, Victor's attraction to metaphysics continues to threaten his modern education. M. Krempe insists that Victor break with alchemy and embrace "modern natural philosophy." Krempe, a product of an "enlightened and scientific age," appears to be a thoroughgoing empiricist, and Victor rejects with "contempt" his study of dingy "realities" unadorned by metaphysical speculation (F, 41).

In pursuit of harmony, Victor finds his intellectual model in M. Waldman, the Romantic scientist who unifies ancient and modern knowledge for Victor. Waldman, as Anne Mellor demonstrates, resembles Humphry Davy, the British chemist whose works Shelley had read just prior to writing *Frankenstein*.[37] According to historian of science D. M. Knight, Davy typifies the Romantic movement in science, especially its grand unifying schemes and resemblance to alchemy:

> The widespread belief in the unity of matter, the view of chemical synthesis as a union of opposites, and the idea, implicit in Davy's *Consolations*, that the researches of the chemist can somehow cast light on the problems of the existence of God, freedom and immortality, all show an affinity with the alchemical scheme of things.[38]

Waldman wins Victor's confidence by affirming Victor's favorite alchemists: "[T]hese were men to whose indefatigable zeal modern philosophers were indebted for most of the foundations of their knowledge" (F, 42–43). In describing Frankenstein's "fatal" education as a reconciliation of chemistry and alchemy, Shelley reflects negatively on the synthesizing impulse of her Romantic peers—especially on the sort of conversation, mixing Gothic German ghost stories and modern galvanic experiments, that engendered her own dream of horror—the dream which, as she recounts in her 1831 preface, inspired *Frankenstein*.

The Krempe–Waldman contrast furnishes another form of haunting similitude as Frankenstein examines each man's "physiognomy," or physical appearance. The pseudoscience of physiognomy held that the body, especially the face and posture, revealed, or was sympathetic to, the moral and emotional constitution. Thus M. Krempe, the materialist, is "a little squat man, with a gruff voice and repulsive countenance" whereas Waldman presents "an aspect expressive of the greatest benevolence," and a "voice the sweetest I had ever heard" (F, 41). Frankenstein makes harmony of body a criterion for the assessment of ideas: of Krempe he says "the teacher did not prepossess me in favour of the doctrine." By his own admission, Frankenstein is highly prejudiced by his "secluded" childhood, full of "old familiar faces," which "had given me invincible repugnance to new countenances" (F, 40). We are prepared then to expect Frankenstein—if he is "repulsed" by the realistic disharmony of Krempe's ideas and appearance—to be incapable of tolerating the disjunctions of his creature.

Notes

12. For a more extended discussion of the problem of sympathy and its relationship to theatricality, see David Marshall, *The Surprising Effects of Sympathy: Marivaux, Diderot, Rousseau, and Mary Shelley* (Chicago: University of Chicago Press, 1988).

13. Ibid., 3.

14. *Oxford English Dictionary*, 2nd edn. (Oxford: Clarendon Press, 1989), s.v. "sympathy."

36. Beth Newman, "Narratives of Seduction and the Seductions of Narrative: The Frame Structure of *Frankenstein*," *ELH* 53.1 (1986): 146.

37. Anne K. Mellor, "*Frankenstein*: A Feminist Critique of Science," in *One Culture: Essays in Science and Literature*, ed. George Levine (Madison: University of Wisconsin Press, 1987), 59.

38. David M. Knight, "The Physical Sciences and the Romantic Movement," *History of Sciences* 9 (1970): 59.

Works by Mary Shelley

History of a Six Weeks' Tour Through a Part of France, Switzerland, Germany and Holland: With Letters Descriptive of a Sail Round the Lake of Geneva, and of the Glaciers of Chamouni, 1817.

Frankenstein: Or, The Modern Prometheus, 1818 (3d edition 1831).

"On Ghosts," 1824.

Valperga, Or, the Life and Adventures of Castruccio, Prince of Lucca, 1823.

"Giovanni Villani," 1823.

"Madame D'Houtetot," 1823.

The Last Man, 1826.

"A Visit to Brighton," 1826.

The Fortunes of Perkin Warbeck, A Romance, 1830.

"Memoir of William Godwin," 1831.

Proserpine, a Mythological Drama in Two Acts, 1831. (first published 1922)

Lodore, 1835.

Lives of the Most Eminent Literary and Scientific Men of Italy, Spain and Portugal, vols. 1 and 2, 1835, vol. 3, 1836.

Falkner, 1837.

Rambles in Germany and Italy, 1844.

Midas!, first published 1922. *Mary Shelley: Collected Tales and Stories,* first published 1976. *Maurice, or the Fisher's Cot,* first published 1998.

Annotated Bibliography

Brennan, Matthew C. "*The Landscape of Grief in Mary Shelley's Frankenstein.*" From *Studies in the Humanities*, vol. 15, no. 1 (June 1988): 33–44.

Discusses how Mary Shelley's attitude toward daydreams and landscape serve as an indication of emotional status. Brennan contrasts Victor Frankenstein's preferences with those of his friend, Henry Clerval, stating that Clerval, the more stable and sociable of the two, delights in the external pleasures of picturesque environment of such places as Oxford, while Victor, who abhors society, finds solace in the sublime landscape of such places as Switzerland that serve as a form of escape.

Caldwell, Janis McLarren. "Science and Sympathy in *Frankenstein.*" From *Literature and Medicine in Nineteenth-Century Britain: From Mary Shelley to George Eliot.* Cambridge, UK and New York: Cambridge University Press (2004): 25–45.

Focusing on the importance of "sympathy" as a major theme in *Frankenstein*, Caldwell sees each narrator in the novel as either yearning for or mourning the loss of a sympathetic relationship. Caldwell explains that the definition of sympathy in Mary Shelley's time is "fellow feeling," and carried two other connotations—magical correspondence and "modern" mechanical communication. Caldwell maintains that Shelley is critiquing these notions of sympathetic communication that required a sameness or identification among the participants in order to affect a sympathetic relationship and calling, instead, for a sympathy based on difference.

Cox, Tracy. "*Frankenstein* and Its Cinematic Translations." From *Critical Essays on Mary Wollstonecraft Shelley.* Edited by Mary Lowe-Evans. New York: G.K. Hall & Co. (1998): 214–29.

Applying Walter Benjamin's theory of translation, Cox compares the complex problems that accompany cinematic versions of the novel to Benjamin's notion of the task of the translator, namely, to recreate the original. Focusing on the issue of "specularity" and the spectacular in *Frankenstein*, Cox discusses three classic film versions: Edison's *Frankenstein* (1910) (the first film adaptation), *Frankenstein* (1931, starring Boris Karloff), and Kenneth Branagh's *Frankenstein* (1994).

Gilbert, Sandra M. and Susan Gubar. "Horror's Twin: Mary Shelley's Monstrous Eve." From *The Madwoman in the Attic: The Woman Writer and the Nineteenth-Century Literary Imagination*. New Haven and London: Yale University Press (2000): 227–47.

Gilbert and Gubar read *Frankenstein* in the context of *Paradise Lost*, focusing on both the solipsistic relationships and the novel's incest-obsession, which they maintain have as much to do with the Miltonic framework as they do to Mary Shelley's life. Within the context of the "moral ambiguity and symbolic slipperiness of all the characterizations," they identify Victor and his monster, as well as the secondary characters, as caught up in a continual duplication and reduplication of roles, a narrative that mocks Milton's epic in its replaying of the neo-biblical roles of *Paradise Lost*.

Griffin, Andrew. "Fire and Ice in *Frankenstein*." From *The Endurance of Frankenstein: Essays on Mary Shelley's Novel*. Edited by George Levine and U.C. Knoepflmacher. Berkeley: University of California Press (1994): 49–73.

Discusses the meaning of fire and ice within the Romantic imagination as symbols of two extremes that are reconciled and unified in the universe of their writings. In *Frankenstein*, these extremes are expressed in several ways, among them Walton's dream of a tropical paradise in the North Pole and the monster's death as suicide-by-fire at the same North Pole. It is Griffin's contention that the monster's desire for the safety and warmth of hearth and home places him within the Victorian notion of domesticity, a middle ground between the two competing emotions—namely, the blaze of passion and the cold stillness that epitomizes an emotional void.

Jordanova, Ludmilla. "Melancholy Reflection: Constructing an Identity for Unveilers of Nature." From *Frankenstein, Creation and Monstrosity*. Edited by Stephen Bann. London: Reaktion Books, Ltd. (1994): 60–76.

Focusing on the definition of melancholy in the early nineteenth century as a word with both medical and general connotations, Jordanova finds it an apt description of Victor Frankenstein's ambivalence toward internal conflicts, evoking both mournful feelings as well as a sense of pleasure and self-indulgence. More specifically as it relates to Victor in his capacity as "scientific overreacher," it is a term that encompasses a wide variety of disciplines that sought to probe the secrets of nature and that has historical implications in that it was a time in which the scientist lacked state support and cultural reward. Jordanova maintains that this leads to a predicament for the scientist who was both a brave explorer hero and a loner doomed to failure.

Ketterer, David. *Frankenstein's Creation: The Book, The Monster, and Human Reality*. Victoria, B.C., Canada: University of Victoria, 1979.

Discusses various structural and metaphorical themes, among them the "book as monster" and "reality as metaphor." As to the first theme, Ketterer sees the imperfect construction and often stilted language of *Frankenstein* as mirroring the disparate materials from which the monster has been fashioned in that Mary Shelley was consciously assembling and arranging diverse materials in the novel. In the second instance, Ketterer sees Shelley as grappling with various questions and uncertainties as to what constitutes the "Other," wherein the monster belongs to a transcendental reality existing "beyond the pale of humanity and nature." Throughout his monograph, Ketterer underscores the vast scope of Shelley's literary and philosophical reading.

Kiely, Robert. *The Romantic Novel in England*. Cambridge, MA: Harvard University Press (1972): 155–173.

Discusses Victor Frankenstein as a romantic hero, whose allure, despite his fatal flaws, resides in his potentiality. Kiely argues that this potentiality is to be found in the depths of his suffering and torment. He further maintains that Victor has the privilege of a type of immunity accorded to scientists and artists, as evidenced by the fact that he dies somewhat unrepentant, indicating that his failed experiment is the result of an accident, rather than an excess of pride.

Levine, George. "The Ambiguous Heritage of *Frankenstein*." From *The Endurance of Frankenstein: Essays on Mary Shelley's Novel*. Edited by George Levine and U.C. Knoepflmacher. Berkeley: University of California Press (1994): 3–30.

Compares the espousal of passivity and acquiescence in Percy Bysshe's *Prometheus Unbound* as a means of triumphing over Jupiter with Mary Shelley's *Frankenstein* in which she created a secular myth of mysterious earthly powers that transform the pagan and Christian traditions. Levine identifies Frankenstein as a modern nineteenth-century myth firmly rooted in the temporality of the material world and presented through the mode of realism—a "secularization of the creation myth"—which has had far-reaching influence on subsequent writers, philosophers, and psychologists.

Mellor, Anne K. *Mary Shelley: Her Life, Her Fiction, Her Monsters*. New York and London: Routledge, 1989.

A biography of Mary Shelley from a feminist perspective, Mellor's argument is that the author exhibits a profound tension inherent in the concept of a bourgeois family, which she promotes in her writing. Mellor analyzes Frankenstein as Mary Shelley's feminist critique of the scientific knowledge of her day, an analysis that also explores the dangerous implications of scientific practices in her time and challenges the prevailing cultural bias that saw nature as inherently female.

Reichardt, Jasia. "Artificial Life and the Myth of Frankenstein." From *Frankenstein, Creation and Monstrosity*. Edited by Stephen Bann. London: Reaktion Books, Ltd. (1994): 136–57.

Discusses the emotive power of the monster, which Reichardt refers to as "Frankenstein," a being at once humane, sympathetic, and endowed with eloquence and learning.

Reichardt maintains that the real tragedy of *Frankenstein* stems from Victor's immediate revulsion by and escape from the sight of his creature, "the result of his inadequate workmanship," rather than his fear that he has unleashed a being he cannot control. In the concluding section of his essay, Reichardt discusses the topic of artificial life as a "collage of existing parts" in which technology can juxtapose images of famous people from completely different times in history that take on a life of their own, thereby creating a myth.

Smith, Crosbie. "Frankenstein and Natural Magic." From *Frankenstein, Creation and Monstrosity*. Edited by Stephen Bann. London: Reaktion Books, Ltd. (1994): 39-59.

Crosbie sees Victor Frankenstein's character as embodying both the "rationality" of Enlightenment thinking and darker aspects of human beings and nature beloved by the Romantic poets and the author herself. In the context of Enlightenment philosophy and its notions of order and stability for both man and nature, Victor comes from a family committed to respectability and public service. However, the darker aspects of his being are manifested by his obsessive pursuit of the "elixir of life," the raising of ghosts, and a fascination with electricity, which passions accord with the spectacular aspects of modern chemistry and an unbridled desire to probe the secrets of nature at all costs.

Spark, Muriel. *Mary Shelley*. New York: E. P. Dutton, 1987.

Spark sees Mary Shelley as having created a new and hybrid fictional species in *Frankenstein*. Though she acknowledges the primacy of Gothic influence in the novel, Spark maintains that Shelley went beyond the conventional props of haunted castles and lurid plots by appealing to the "speculation of the mind," stating that *Frankenstein*'s theme of scientific proposition is precisely that which transforms an otherwise Gothic tale into a new genre of substance.

Thornburg, Mary K. Patterson. *The Monster in the Mirror: Gender and the Sentimental/Gothic Myth in Frankenstein.* Ann Arbor, Michigan: UMI Research Press, 1984.

Explores how the sentimental/Gothic myth, which depicted a world with inherent contradictions, gradually evolved and took shape in *Frankenstein*. Thornburg defines this particular myth against its earlier traditions as essentially secular in nature, relating specifically to the middle class, seemingly realistic in his literary representation of contemporary life, and incorporating disparate elements from the Gothic and sentimental traditions, this last characteristic being a combination of a masculine and a feminine consciousness. Among other things, Thornburg sees the Gothic tragedy of Victor and his monster set against the sentimentally rendered De Lacey family.

Veeder, William. *Mary Shelley and Frankenstein: The Fate of Androgyny.* Chicago and London: The University of Chicago Press, 1986. © 1986 by The University of Chicago.

Sees the characterization of Victor Frankenstein and Robert Walton as marked by a bifurcation in gender traits wherein the masculine ambition for daring and bold scientific experimentation is balanced by feminine traits such as sympathetic concern for human welfare and affectionate feelings toward Elizabeth and Margaret. Veeder maintains that Mary Shelley's intention in Frankenstein is to show how a split psyche attempts to heal itself through the creation of a monster.

Contributors

Harold Bloom is Sterling Professor of the Humanities at Yale University. He is the author of 30 books, including *Shelley's Mythmaking*, *The Visionary Company*, *Blake's Apocalypse*, *Yeats*, *A Map of Misreading*, *Kabbalah and Criticism*, *Agon: Toward a Theory of Revisionism*, *The American Religion*, *The Western Canon*, and *Omens of Millennium: The Gnosis of Angels, Dreams, and Resurrection*. *The Anxiety of Influence* sets forth Professor Bloom's provocative theory of the literary relationships between the great writers and their predecessors. His most recent books include *Shakespeare: The Invention of the Human*, a 1998 National Book Award finalist, *How to Read and Why*, *Genius: A Mosaic of One Hundred Exemplary Creative Minds*, *Hamlet: Poem Unlimited*, *Where Shall Wisdom Be Found?*, and *Jesus and Yahweh: The Names Divine*. In 1999, Professor Bloom received the prestigious American Academy of Arts and Letters Gold Medal for Criticism. He has also received the International Prize of Catalonia, the Alfonso Reyes Prize of Mexico, and the Hans Christian Andersen Bicentennial Prize of Denmark.

Janyce Marson is a doctoral student at New York University. She is writing a dissertation of the rhetoric of the mechanical in Wordsworth, Coleridge, and Mary Shelley.

Percy Bysshe Shelley was the husband of Mary Shelley and one of the canonical Romantic poets and literary critics. Among his chief works that influenced *Frankenstein* are his lyrical drama, *Prometheus Unbound*, and his poem, "Mutability."

Crosbie Smith has been Professor of the History of Science at the University of Kent, Canterbury. He is the author of *The Science of Energy: A Cultural History of Energy Physics in Victorian Britain*, and coauthor of *Energy and Empire: A Biographical Study of Lord Kelvin*.

Ludmilla Jordanova has been Professor of Visual Arts, School of World Art Studies and Museology at the University of East

Anglia, and Dean of the School of World Art Studies and Music. She is the author of *Nature Displayed: Gender, Science, and Medicine, 1769–1820: Essays* and coauthor of *The Quick and the Dead: Artists and Anatomy.*

Anne K. Mellor is Distinguished Professor of English at the University of California at Los Angeles. She is the author of *Mothers of the Nation: Women's Political Writing in England, 1780–1830, Romanticism & Gender*, and *English Romantic Irony.*

David Ketterer is Professor Emeritus of English at Concordia University. He is the author of *Canadian Science Fiction and Fantasy, Edgar Allan Poe: Life, Work and Criticism*, and *Imprisoned in a Tesseract: The Life and Work of James Blish.*

Muriel Spark (1918–2006) was a leading Scottish novelist of modern times who wrote more than twenty novels during her long career. She received the U.S. Ingersoll Foundation T.S. Eliot Award in 1992 and the British Literature Prize in 1997. She became Dame Commander of the Order of the British Empire in 1993, in recognition of her services to literature. Her novels include *The Prime of Miss Jean Brodie, The Comforters*, and *Aiding and Abetting*. She was also a coeditor of *My Best Mary*, a selection of letters of Mary Wollstonecraft Shelley.

Sandra M. Gilbert has been Professor of English at the University of California, Davis. Along with Susan Gubar, she has published *The Madwoman in the Attic: The Woman Writer and the Nineteenth-Century Literary Imagination* in 1979, a runner-up for both the Pulitzer Prize and the National Book Critics Circle Award. Gilbert is the author of a prose memoir, *Wrongful Death: A Medical Tragedy*, and many books of poetry, including *Ghost Volcano, Inventions of Farewell: A Book of Elegies*, and *Kissing the Bread: New and Selected Poems.*

Susan Gubar has been Distinguished Professor of English and Women's Studies at Indiana University. Along with Sandra M. Gilbert, she published *The Madwoman in the Attic: The Woman*

Writer and the Nineteenth-Century Literary Imagination in 1979, a runner-up for both the Pulitzer Prize and the National Book Critics Circle Award. Gilbert and Gubar also coauthored *No Man's Land: The Place of the Woman Writer in the Twentieth Century; The War of the Words, Sexchanges,* and *Letters from the Front.* Gubar is the author *of Racechanges: White Skin, Black Face in American Culture,* and the editor of *Critical Condition: Feminism at the Turn of the Century.*

Laura P. Claridge has taught at the United States Naval Academy. She is the author of *Romantic Potency: The Paradox of Desire* and *Norman Rockwell: A Life.*

Betty T. Bennett is Distinguished Professor of Literature at American University. She is the author of *Mary Wollstonecraft Shelley: An Introduction, Lives of the Great Romantics III: Godwin, Wollstonecraft & Mary Shelley by Their Contemporaries,* and an editor of *Shelley: Poet and Legislator of the World.*

Matthew Brennan has been Professor of English at Indiana State University. He is the author of "Coleridge, Friedrich, and the 'Hymn' to Mountain Glory," and *Wordsworth, Turner, and Romantic Landscape: A Study of the Picturesque and the Sublime.*

William Crisman has been an Associate Professor of English, Comparative Literature, and German at Pennsylvania State University, Altoona. He is the author of *The Crises of "Language and Dead Signs" in Ludwig Tieck's Prose Fiction.*

Janis McLarren Caldwell has been an Assistant Professor of English at the University of California, Santa Barbara. She is the author of "Narrating Pictures: Victorian Ekphrastic Poetry and the Ethics of Comparison."

Acknowledgments

"On *Frankenstein*" by Percy Bysshe Shelley. From *Frankenstein: The 1818 Text Contexts, Nineteenth-Century Responses, Modern Criticism*. (A Norton Critical Edition): 185. © 1996 by W.W. Norton & Company. Originally published in *The Athenaeum Journal of Literature, Science and the Fine Arts*, Nov. 10, 1832. Reprinted by permission.

"Frankenstein and Natural Magic" by Crosbie Smith. From *Frankenstein: Creation and Monstrosity*. Edited by Stephen Bann. London: Reaktion Books (1994): 41–44. © 1994 by Reaktion Books. Reprinted by permission.

"Melancholy Reflection: Constructing an Identity for Unveilers of Nature" by Ludmilla Jordanova. From *Frankenstein: Creation and Monstrosity*. Edited by Stephen Bann. London: Reaktion Books (1994): 60–63. © 1994 by Reaktion Books. Reprinted by permission.

"Promethean Politics" by Anne K. Mellor. From *Mary Shelley: Her Life, Her Fiction, Her Monsters*. New York and London: Routledge (1989): 70–74. © 1989 by Routledge, Chapman and Hall, Inc. Reprinted by permission.

" 'Spirit of Life': Metaphoric Nexus" by David Ketterer. From *Frankenstein's Creation: The Book, The Monster, and Human Reality*. Victoria, B.C., Canada: University of Victoria (1979): 67–71. © 1979 by David Ketterer. Reprinted by permission.

"Frankenstein" by Muriel Spark. From *Mary Shelley*. New York: E.P. Dutton (1987): 161–165. © 1987 by Copyright Administration Limited. Reprinted by permission.

"Horror's Twin: Mary Shelley's Monstrous Eve" by Sandra M. Gilbert and Susan Gubar. From *The Madwoman in the Attic: The Woman Writer and the Nineteenth-Century Literary*

Index

Characters in literary works are indexed by first name (if any), followed by the name of the work in parentheses.